# Job
## DEFENSE
## OF HONOR

# Job
# DEFENSE
# OF HONOR

Roger N. Carstensen

ABINGDON PRESS
NEW YORK—NASHVILLE

JOB: DEFENSE OF HONOR

Acknowledgement is hereby made for permission to use quotations from the following copyrighted material:

From the plays of Euripides, translated by Edward P. Coleridge, published by G. Bell & Sons, Ltd.

From the plays of Aeschylus, translated by Geoffrey Cookson, published by Blackwell's.

From Sophocles, *Philoctetes, Antigone, Trachinae,* and *Electra,* translated by Sir R. C. Jebb, published by Cambridge University Press.

Scripture quotations are from the Revised Standard Version of the Bible, copyrighted 1946 and 1952 by the Division of Christian Education, National Council of Churches, and are used by permission.

SET UP, PRINTED, AND BOUND BY THE PARTHENON PRESS, AT NASHVILLE, TENNESSEE, UNITED STATES OF AMERICA

To my
FATHER and
MOTHER

# Preface

        It is my contention that the frame of reference of the Book of Job is strikingly similar to that of many ancient Greek writers. Whether there is dependence either way is not the purpose of this book to decide. The profound debt owed by modern Western thought to both the Hebrew and Greek heritages suggests why the Book of Job, should it indeed prove a sort of bridge between these two streams of culture, appeals so powerfully to thoughtful people today. References from Greek dramatists and philosophers (Aeschylus, Sophocles, Euripides, Plato, and Aristotle) will be inserted from time to time in appropriate places in the book as uniquely appropriate commentary on Joban themes.

R. N. C.

# Contents

# I

# The Vocabulary of Honor

> The wise hold that everything which depends
> on necessity is its slave.  —Euripides *Orestes*, p. 399

A Japanese general on Okinawa, his forces decisively beaten, retires to his room and, according to hallowed precepts, takes his own life. An insurance salesman mortgages his home and cashes the bonds set aside for his son's education to pay a gambling debt to a business acquaintance. Two men with pistols pace away from each other in a forest clearing; they turn and fire together. One is wounded; satisfied, they leave the clearing reconciled.

These three disconnected experiences have one thing in common: an attempt to defend honor. The general cannot continue to live in a world where his honor has been compromised. He takes his life as one already dead. The insurance salesman pays a debt of honor which overrides all legal and practical obligations. Devolving directly upon his own integrity, it confronts him with greater threats than punishment or want. The duelists, in a clash of interests, have impugned each other's honor; their willingness to risk their lives, whether they win or not, reasserts the existence of their honor and allows them to be friends again.

The history of honor is a history of strength. From the standpoint of general welfare, it is true that the demands of

11

honor have been at times terribly destructive. Feuds and senseless wars provide some of the darkest pages of history. But honor always insists there is a value beyond that of life. It provides an inward strength which overwhelms all other considerations and insists on the ultimate worth of a person within himself. In this sense at least mankind perpetually contradicts Satan's knowledgeable assertion in the Book of Job, "Skin for skin! All that a man has he will give for his life" (2:4).

As a man conceives it, honor does not derive from security, status, or pleasure; it operates in mystery. Some inner, intangible standard of right, established in conscience as undeniable beyond question, lays its stern demand upon the will.

Indeed, it could plausibly be argued that honor simply represents man's attempt to project his own self-created image upon his community. Handling himself as though he were somebody, he persuades his society that he really exists, and feeds his starveling ego with the applause of others.

Sooner or later, however, the demands of honor will compromise reputation. Those in whose opinions a man finds reassurance of his own worth demand, perhaps without intending to do so, that he act against his own sense of justice. If it is not truly inward, honor will then retreat to the shifting, sensible, olive-drab ramparts of prudence, there to be discarded in favor of reputation. He whose moral energy is founded only upon the opinions of others cannot properly use the vocabulary of honor, however just his actions may be in themselves.

Since people may acquire standards of honor which, as in some codes of retaliation, may senselessly endanger whole communities, a sense of honor does not necessarily contribute to general welfare. On the other hand, superior codes of conduct imposed by custom and law but not supported by the inward strength of honor cannot be satisfactorily enforced. In their inevitable self-interest men tend to rationalize themselves away from codes of conduct valuable only to the general good but repressive for the individual. Man needs to be able to support the general good with the demand and the passion of personal honor.

It is of the nature of honor that it not be created to serve an end, but transmitted in a tradition. This is why people are suspicious of the newly rich, and why sons have status superior to employees. When one contrives his own image, the frailty and inconsistency of the self shows through. No ring of sound hardness is there, no genuine luster. Honor cannot be conjured up by clenched fist and gritting teeth; it rests on real foundations. It derives from the value of man in himself, granted from a power transcending him but permitting him to act as a free being. Man is of worth for which no coin is minted; only the brightness of honor can reflect the value of persons.

The Book of Job asserts the worth of man. This worth is not the capacity to produce goods or to improve the face of the world. Man is not valued as a thinker, a philanthropist, or a practicer of religion, although Job is all three. In the Book of Job, man is valued for what he is within himself.

For a man to have value within himself demands integrity, which in a technical sense is to say he is one whole person. He is not a combination of persons, presenting different faces at different times. Whatever the external values a nonintegrated person might represent, he could scarcely have worth in himself because, not being able to remain one person, he really has no consistent identity at all.

While it is possible that an individual have integrity in the sense of unity of character and still not be a good person, the word integrity implies honesty and reliability.

13

It is presumed that a man inwardly whole is such because he recognizes a standard beyond himself to which he submits the wavering forces of his own self-interest.

In a very special way, therefore, the integrity of a man becomes an assertion of a general order of things that is good and true. By the same token, the appearance of a truly evil person, insofar as he shows no evidences of self-destruction in a clash with the general good, threatens the hypothesis of an underlying moral order in human affairs. If it may be shown that a man integrated in his evil prospers because he participates in a society similarly integrated, the attack becomes more powerful. It begins to appear that the whole world is out of step or that goodness is not grounded in reality.

On the other hand, if a man lives in an ordered society where responsibility and truthfulness are respected and rewarded, his life may indicate an integrity which simply reflects the unity of his society. Not being tested, a man's inner weakness, his lack of strong identity, may not become apparent to himself or others. Such a man is in serious personal jeopardy, for the first real challenge to his comfortable set of values may threaten not only his possessions and attainments but his very identity. He is in danger of losing his soul, because he misunderstands himself and has simplified and sentimentalized the world in which he lives. Sophocles says a model of piety may be in unsuspected peril. "He who stands clear of trouble should beware of dangers; and when a man lives at ease, then it is that he should look most closely to his life, lest ruin come on it by stealth." (*Philoctetes*, p. 186.)

In a sense integrity is a private matter in that it represents the worth of a man within himself. Man is, however, essentially social, and his integrity has to be expressed in human relationships. When he thinks of himself as being under an inner obligation to act consistently and constructively toward others, thus expressing his integrity, he is likely to use the term "honor." The honorable thing to do is that which expresses one's integrity in actions involving others, whatever the results may be. An honorable man does not conceive that any event can justify the sacrifice of integrity, for this would destroy his identity.

Honor, as a word in the vocabulary, represents not only how a man sees himself but how others see him. The man who learns, thinks, and lives as a unit of a group finds it almost impossible to separate these two uses of the word. When someone is said to gain honor, it is generally supposed that his reputation has improved. That he himself has improved does not necessarily follow, for the reason that others may not value integrity highly.

Aristotle insists that all men strive for honor—meaning honors externally bestowed. "Men seem to pursue honour in order that they may be assured of their goodness." (*Nicomachean Ethics*, p. 341.) Men who have no inner conviction of spiritual worth lose their identity; they therefore seek it from society. The approval of one's peers becomes more than a source of satisfaction and pleasure; it becomes a creature necessity. One way to demand the respect of others is to accumulate possessions. Aristotle says, "Desert is relative to external goods." (*Ibid.*, p. 370.) Possessions become symbols of man's value in himself— that is, of his honor.

He who establishes his reputation externally as a means of asserting his inward worth develops a profound anxiety because the very center of his being is, as it were, outside himself. He tries to ingratiate himself everywhere and ends up belonging nowhere. At one and the same time he despises and depends upon those from whom he has bribed the gestures of approval and respect.

One does not have to seek the external symbols of honor to be threatened by them. Being consistent within itself, honor is strong. In the order of things, strength tends to be rewarded. The Jains of India in past times gained an extraordinary capacity for honesty because of their contempt for earthly possessions; free from them, they could be honest with them. Being honest they were trusted as merchants. Indirectly, therefore, the integrity that found goods unnecessary contributed to the acquiring of goods, making Jains one of the wealthy classes in India. Thus, honorable men frequently heap around themselves the unsolicited spoils of their strength. At the same time, they may be seduced by their own success into confounding the symbols of worth with worth itself. Like the rich man of Jesus' parable, the only self they know is the one attached to much goods. Take away the barns, and the self vanishes into nothingness. (Cf. Luke 12:13-21.)

Men therefore face the task of believing themselves to be of worth in spite of outward evidences that they are! One must not belong to his possessions; he is able to possess them because their detachment does not threaten him. Otherwise, he would not be able to dispense with them and could not control them. Not controlling them, he could not own them. Similarly, one must not be a slave of reputation; otherwise, mirroring community opinion, he possesses no convictions of his own. The apostle Paul expresses similar views when he says in effect that all things are ours so long as we are Christ's. (Cf. I Cor. 3:21-23.) The Power beyond is the sole dependable basis upon which man can save himself from being strangled by his own success.

The councils of heaven are interested in the honor of man because it asserts spiritual power. Only in man's free choice of the righteousness of heaven can that righteousness stand in itself. Just as honorable acts coerced by profit or fear are honorable no longer, a righteousness of heaven imposed on man by overt sanctions loses its proper character. If Job serves God for nothing, or beyond this if he serves him in spite of everything, he asserts the sovereignty of a Force that moves independently of coercion. Human integrity supports not only the dignity of persons sound in their freedom, but the majesty of a God whose will is done without compulsion!

The Book of Job becomes not only a search for the honor of man, but for that of God. When the question is raised in the prologue whether there can be a human righteousness apart from material coercion toward it, the question can also be raised, as it is in the poetry, whether God can be considered just apart from cosmic power. Take away the wind, the fire, and the earthquake—all the implacable forces of the natural world—and what is left of the righteousness-in-itself, or honor, of God? Will his ways be approved by honest men if they are examined in their own merits?

God himself is without honor if he relies upon phenomenal power, beyond his own essential spiritual nature, to coerce man to reproduce within himself the divine character. Does not God's goodness exist in and of itself? Does he not trust it to emerge in the freedom of man?

On the other hand, if the goodness of man is his response to a divine law which is supported by the irresistible power of God's blessings and punishments, is not man still the creature of his own environment? *God* becomes simply the inescapable essence of environment. The honor of man becomes as inevitable as heat following friction. A man of formally irreproachable character may be without inward honor; for the moment that he encounters what appears to be a force greater than God, he will at once alter the conduct of his life to satisfy his new master. Even if he never meets such a force, and thus remains irreproachable to the end, his righteousness never attains the status of honor. Should God force man to a pattern of righteousness, however correct the pattern may seem to be in a strategy of history, the honor of man would be decisively compromised.

The only way that man may submit to the will of God as the basic source of his honor without imperiling that honor is to do so in freedom. He identifies God with the right-in-itself and holds fast in spite of consequences.

From this point of view, the assertion of the honor of God and that of man is really one process. This process is simply to demonstrate that a man may retain his integrity—that is, his honor as it is within himself—within what seems to be a disintegrating moral universe. He therefore testifies to a power in his Creator that is spiritual, beyond the rationale of phenomenal cause and effect. Thus the honor of God, too, is justified.

The Book of Job sets out, in the prologue, to show that authentic honor is a possibility for moral giants. In the dialogue it dares the greater task of showing how, in the grace of God, honor is a possibility for Everyman.

# III

# The Prologue: The Curtain Rises

> Heavens! My dear Glaucon . . . how ener-
> getically you polish them up for the decision, first one and
> then the other, as if they were two statues.
> —Plato *The Republic*, p. 312

In the second book of Plato's republic, Glaucon, the pupil
of Socrates, asks whether there can be such a thing as
pure justice in the experience of man. He asserts that man
acts only from selfish motives and that he upholds standards of just conduct only when it is to his profit. Much that
passes for justice is mere show, covering a cynical disregard for the rights of others. Many men are coerced
by law or self-interest into the practice of righteousness.
"All men who practise justice do so against their will, of
necessity, but not as a good." (*Ibid.*, p. 311.) To speak
of real justice, Glaucon concludes, is to speak of justice
apart from coercion. "I want to hear justice praised in
respect of itself." (*Ibid.*)

In order to praise justice "in respect of itself" Glaucon
visualizes, on one hand, a man who is absolutely unjust
at the same time thought to be perfectly just. This wicked
man would be the recipient of all the favors of earth and
heaven. On the other hand, he visualizes a man perfectly
just, but supposed by the rest of the world to be unjust.

"Let him be the best of men, and let him be thought the worst; then he will have been put to the proof; and we shall see whether he will be affected by the fear of infamy and its consequences." (*Ibid.*, p. 312.) Glaucon goes on to insist that the just man be tortured. He will be "scourged, racked, bound—will have his eyes burnt out; and, at last, after suffering every kind of evil, he will be impaled." (*Ibid.*) Such a man must conclude that justice does not pay.

While Glaucon intended to show that justice in itself, minus all rewards, contributed not at all to human happiness and thus was not "good," the hypothesis he created to prove his point beautifully describes the idea structure of the prologue to Job. The prologue does not set out to demonstrate the *superiority* but the *possibility* of absolute justice. Glaucon's hypothesis is incarnate in a man who, while he is the best of his generation, is at the same time the most accursed.

Whether justice in itself is a good is, however, dealt with in the Book of Job. The most obvious answer is in the epilogue, where the restored sufferer is repaid double for his material losses and given a new and presumably superior family. (Cf. 42:10-17.) The more profound answer, which is very near the center of interest in this book, is in the poetry, which will be dealt with subsequently.

The ease with which one can thus move from the classic Greek thought-world to that of Job helps prepare the mind for the degree to which Aeschylus, Sophocles, and Euripedes, the triumvirate of classic Greek tragedy, may serve as ideological commentators upon the biblical drama. This drama addresses itself to the same frightening phenomenon as that confronting the Greeks: the emerging of a new man, tragic in his individuality, gripped by a fate from which he could not free himself and to which he could not be reconciled.

Within the Book of Job itself the function of the prologue is to lay the background for the treatment of the
problem of the justice of God by introducing the story of
a righteous sufferer. The problem is thrown into bold
relief to the extent that contrasts in Job's condition are
emphasized. The simple, classic outlines of the old story
explore the highest pinnacles of happiness and lowest
depths of despair. The introduction therefore can be described as both an attack upon and a defense of human
worth. It is an attempt to find out what man is in himself.

Scene one: Job, a sheik in the land of Uz, is a righteous man, a moral giant of his time. He is also the richest
of all the sons of the East, possessing incalculable riches in
servants, flocks, and herds. He has ten children—seven
sons and three daughters. He is deeply religious. When
his children celebrate their birthdays together, Job, fear-
ing that the stimulations of a party might lead the young to
some dangerous irreverence, offers intercessory sacrifices
for them. Modern parents easily understand why this
ancient partiarch sought the smoke of sacrifice as a shield
between God's searching eyes and the playfulness of his
children!

Job represents the ideal of practical religion. Simulta-
neously holy and affluent, he illustrates what to ancient
Hebrew and modern Christian the word *blessed* ought to
mean. The book therefore begins with a picture proper to
the end of any moralizing play, where, all difficulties re-
solved, good people live happily ever after. Indeed, the
author is under some difficulty when he tries to show that
Job is better off at the end. Doubling his possessions is
something like comparing a two-billionaire to a one-bil-
lionaire, and the vaunted beauty of the last three daughters hardly compensated for the slaughter of the original ten
children.

Scene two: the stage shifts precipitately from earth to

heaven. The sons of God are assembled in convocation before the divine Presence. Perhaps they are about to carry forth a discussion of pressing problems of earth, such as was done in the scene described by Micaiah to Ahab and Jehoshaphat in I Kings 22.

Suddenly Satan stands among them. While we know that at this point "the adversary" appears as one of the servants of God, we probably will not be able to avoid seeing him as the "devil" of later centuries. With red eyes and Mephistophelian beard he towers, spreading great bat wings. Arms akimbo, he confronts the heavenly congregation, teeth bared in an insulting, sneering smile. Above the throng, God sits in imperturbable self-sufficiency. Throwing his mantle about him, the fiend stalks down the hallway suddenly created by the shrinking angels until he stands before the throne.

After a moment of Miltonic silence God speaks. "Where have you been, Satan?" Glowing with infernal satisfaction, Satan guardedly replies, "Up and down in the earth, and back and forth in it." Translated into modern idiom, he is saying, "I've been getting around. . . . You name it, I've been there." Those who attribute all human mischief to Satan's stimulation must certainly agree with this laconic description! "Surely then," God responds, "you have encountered Job." God describes Job as a blameless man, excellently representative, apparently, of what heaven considers pious men should be. (Cf. 1:8.)

Satan immediately senses the challenge implicit in God's assertion. In effect, he responds, "Yeah, I've seen him. . . . Huh! Mama's little boy! Teacher's pet! I'm not impressed! You have showered every blessing on him; you have built a hedge around him so that he cannot be harmed. Of course he's righteous! Who wouldn't be?" Satan himself would undoubtedly be pious were it this profitable! His challenge: "Take from him all he has, and he will curse you to your face." All that Satan had to say of Job is summarized in a simple, mocking line: "Will Job serve God for nothing?" (Cf. 1:9-11.)

However Satan is costumed, in whatever key his role is played, the issue is clear. The worth of man is brought into question. Since Job is the best man his times can produce, to discredit him is to discredit humanity. A minor deity bent upon protecting the honor of his creature (and hence his own) might have found countless devices by which to shield him from prying celestials. He might have said, "Shut up!" or "Meeting dismissed" or "Gabriel, give the benediction!" He might simply have vaporized Satan on the spot, erasing the incident from cherubic memory. On the other hand, while permitting the test, he might so have forearmed Job as to leave Satan (unaware of the warning) completely baffled by Job's triumphant endurance.

But God accepts the challenge on Satan's terms. What a colossal risk! Genesis was frightening enough! There God made man in his own image, and set him loose in a paradise with a built-in booby trap! But the Book of Job is even more daring. Living in an oasis of human happiness in partnership with God, apparent conqueror of the human weakness which drove the primal pair from Eden, Job is flung capriciously from paradise to hell. Only the Partner whom he trusts has the capacity to do this to him. What will he say? What will he do?

Keeper of his own counsel, God lets the problem form itself in the living laboratory of Job's heart. He removes the protective hedge and with it the whole moral system of retribution to which Job and his peers have geared their lives. A series of sweeping catastrophes hammers Job's prosperity into ashes, leaving him bankrupt and bereft. Messengers of disaster, treading on one another's heels, pant out their dread tidings, announcing at the last the death of the children for whom he has just been praying.

41

Having been highly exalted, Job is susceptible to a tragic downfall. "For when a man of high degree meets with adversity, he feels the strangeness of his fallen state more keenly than a sufferer of long standing." (Euripedes *Helen*, p. 301.)

The image of stalwart faithfulness with which the story began is never changed. So far as the prologue is concerned, Job is vindicated. Drawing from an immense inner strength, he remains unshaken. "Naked I came from my mother's womb, and naked shall I return; The Lord gave, and the Lord has taken away; Blessed be the name of the Lord." (1:21.)

Following Job's initial triumph, the opening scene in heaven is abruptly repeated. Into the heavenly assembly returns Satan; the Lord pointedly reminds him of Job's vindication, in his steadfastness, of the hopes of heaven. The adversary cries, "Foul! You did not get down to what really matters! Let me get my hands on *him!* All that a man has he will give for his life!" God accepts the ultimate challenge, allowing Satan to torture Job bodily. However, his life cannot be taken.

Suddenly Job is afflicted by painful ulcers which break out all over his body. His community, convinced by the magnitude of his trials that he is under the special censure of God, rejects him; he sits among ashes (probably the community garbage dump) and prepares for death. His wife, horrified by his agony, believing that his misery is simply prolonged by his stubborn refusal to deny the God who has stricken him, urges him to "curse God, and die." Job indignantly rejects her proposal, and does not "sin [against God] with his lips" (2:9-10).

Whether he (or heaven) knows it or not, Job has not drained the dregs of his cup of suffering. His three friends, who prove in their blundering good intentions to be Satan's most effective minions, put in an appearance. Probing with spears sharper than those of torturing demons, they rake over the ashes of Job's hopes until they have uncovered and quenched every ember. The subsequent dialogue is an emphatic reminder that man's most profound anguish is mediated to him by his fellows, who, while indispensable to his spiritual survival, are nevertheless a profound threat to it.

The question under the outlines of this old story emerges very distinctly: Does "disinterested righteousness" really exist? Phrased today, the question might read, If there were no heaven, would you be a Christian? If extinction were your inevitable end, would you accept the disciplines of the Christian religion?

Beyond this, the poetry will raise the questions, Will a man remain righteous when pain and disgrace seem to be the result of his goodness? Will a man go to hell for the glory of God?

To Satan's question, "Will Job serve God for nothing?" there emerges a positive answer. "Yes! Yes! Precisely so! Job *will* serve God for nothing!" It is only on this basis that righteousness is fundamentally different from informed selfishness.

The prologue to Job begins with a picture of human happiness fundamentally attractive to all generations. In the person of Job, spiritual and temporal worth unite in the superlative richness of good living on earth. He is no ascetic, seeking beatitude in the abandonment of tangible things. Neither is he a libertine, justifying his existence in careless irresponsibility, in heedless, lusty, animal pleasure. Job represents the sainthood of good sense; the life of sound men under the care of an intelligent, responsible God. Human honor and divine favor become two sides of the same coin.

While the prologue asks, in a debate that takes place in heaven, whether there is a truly righteous man, the

43

dialogue asks, in a debate carried on by man, whether there can be a truly righteous God. So long as God the Creator embodies high purpose in men, his status is critically involved in the events of history. To the Jew, man is the pinnacle of creation. To reduce man to a cipher is to render the cosmos meaningless.

Job is vindicated in the prologue. Satan's terms are essentially met. It was not a condition of the trial that it be interminable; the penalties were imposed and endured. The introductory story asserts that man *is* capable of enduring deprivation and grief without the loss of his creaturely perspective. Man's identity as one derived from a Creator, whom to serve is his real vocation, emerges from the crucible of suffering fundamentally unchanged. Job *is somebody* in the sense that his praise of God is unmodified by trial, proving that as a person he does not exist simply as the embodiment of predictable creature responses.

Glaucon's proposition has been clearly stated. The ideally good man, tested with laboratory thoroughness, has emerged with undefiled honor. But is this polished hypothesis, this unblemished nobility, real? Is the laboratory of Uz really the fairyland of Oz, with a wizard for a God? Let the question be asked of history and general experience. What does actual man—the kind of man I know and the kind of man I am—say?

Stimulated by the silent presence of his friends and by the reflections of seven days and nights of unremitted anguish, Job steps across the gulf between what ought to be and what is. Every reader pauses with the shock of Job's first strident, discordant outcry.

> Let the day perish wherein I was born,
> and the night which said,
> "A man-child is conceived."
>
> —3:3

Every reader recognizes under the conventions of art the litany of his own darkest hours. "I wish I were dead!" Every reader therefore receives in these lines his first premonition of the ultimate identity of Job.

The prologue to Job is really the raising of a curtain; the play is about to begin.

# IV

# The Dialogue:
# The Fitful Winds of Discourse

SEMI-CHORUS I:    Thou speak'st of the gods as if they were
                  just.
SEMI-CHORUS II:   For who but they allot whate'er betides?
SEMI-CHORUS I:    I see many a contradiction in their deal-
                  ings with men.
SEMI-CHORUS II:   The former fear hath warped thy judg-
                  ment. Vengeance calls vengeance forth;
                  slaughter calls for slaughter, but the gods
                  give respite from affliction, holding in their
                  own hands each thing's allotted end.
                  —Euripides *The Suppliants*, p. 263

Drama demands movement. One of the reasons why the
modern mind finds it difficult to conceive of Job as drama
—and indeed why it may not be drama—is its lack of action.
There may, however, once have been stage directions
which, being known, would modify one's impressions a bit.
There probably was a literary form of which Job is the only
surviving representative; such a work may have involved
formal, classical patterns of action. In any event, we do not
have such stage directions.

There are indeed evidences of action and violence in the
dialogue itself. In 5:2 Eliphaz observes that vexation kills

the fool (probably a reference to Job), and in his second speech he says,

> Why does your heart carry you away,
> and why do your eyes flash?
> —15:12

Bildad accuses Job of tearing himself in his anger (18:4). So Job must have been a pretty active speaker. He himself has promised that he would speak "in the anguish of my spirit" (7:11).

On one occasion the friends apparently prepared to leave him.

> But now, be pleased to look at me;
> for I will not lie to your face.
> Turn, I pray, let no wrong be done.
> Turn now, my vindication is at stake.
> —6:28-29

Again, they apparently interrupt him, and he retorts,

> Let me have silence, and I will speak
> and let come on me what may.
> —13:13

There are numerous other indications that the lines of the dialogue must be read with passion. Raised voices, wild gesticulation, and the nose-to-nose harangue were all probably characteristic of a presentation of Job.

The real movement of the dialogue is, however, psychological and ideological.

> Betwixt him and the man he meets is enmity,
> And in the smiting of their shields shall clash
> Opposing deities.
> —Aeschylus *Seven Against Thebes*, p. 32

47

This development is not easy to trace, because it is not regular and symmetrical. Some generalizations may be helpful.

Job's mood begins in pathos and despair, moves into outrage, and hardens into resolution. The friends begin with a show of comfort, proceed into innuendo and inference, and emerge into outright accusation. At first Job addresses his friends in search of pity; then, debating with the friends, from time to time he addresses his pleas heavenward. Finally, abandoning discussion with the friends, he presents a challenge to God.

There is little real development of the friends' argument. Most of the movement of ideas is in Job himself. By and large, he takes on moral and psychological strength with every word he utters.

The friends represent the forces of traditionalism, conservatism, and dogmatism. They speak with the authority of the past. They are unwilling to jeopardize the comfortable creed of their fathers to make room for a Job whose fate, by his definition, violates the possibilities allowed by the creed. Eliphaz and his committee represent the force of community opinion and community righteousness. They are the voice of the implacable majority and, naturally, of God. They hardly need to develop arguments.

On the other hand, Job represents all those whose experience violates a faith once held. He has found out that words and dogmas satisfactory for solving theoretical problems may actually intensify personal crisis. He has lost his stake in the intrenched moralism of his day. Either a religion is real, so that it provides answers that work, or it is irrelevant, beneath the consideration of serious men. Fighting for his honor and his sanity, Job wants something to happen—right now!

The function of the friends is to provide opportunity for a dialogue. Little as they apparently contribute to Job, their questions and responses are better than for him to mutter to himself. Without them, Job may never have felt himself forced to search for the *Deus abscondus,* the familiar companion of his autumn days who had vanished from His sky as Job's possessions vanished from the earth.

### THE ABSENCE OF GOD

When a city falls
The Gods forsake their ancient habitations.
—Aeschylus *Seven Against Thebes,* p. 29

The dialogue is conducted in the absence of God, who cannot render any comfort to Job without breaking the conditions of the trial. The God whom Job has known moves off his throne. The God who loved righteous people, the God who controlled the moral universe in human history as he controlled the wheeling systems of infinite heaven is no more. True, Job continues to believe in him; he does not have the capacity not to believe. The catastrophes which have crushed him are so bitter, the sorrow which obsesses him is so profound, that he cannot assign it to accident. It hurts too much. There must be a Somebody or a Something behind his anguish. It is not the existence but rather the changed nature of God which seems to be Job's problem.

The absence of God is not therefore a vacuum; it is a fearful new Presence. When Job is struck by disasters, the coincidence and fury of the mysterious plagues are beyond question evidence of their supernatural origin. God has a strange face, mediated by the savagery of Job's experiences.

Job becomes an alien in the midst of familiar things. Catastrophes, even small ones, are able to evoke a feeling of lostness. At the first of the month, when funds run out and one important bill remains to be paid, the householder suddenly has a feeling of panic. "My wife spends too much money. The kids are not studying as they should. How can

49

I ever fix this house up? When will I ever get a raise? The church is full of hypocrites. We are losing the cold war!" Only one thing has really gone wrong, but suddenly everything else is wrong, too, and he finds himself anxious, frustrated.

The extraordinary predicament of Job is not intended to lift him out of the experience of ordinary man. His catastrophes simply represent in the objective world that which occurs subjectively in one's own universe when tragedy strikes. The human body feels only the sharpest of competing pains. Agony tends to be ultimate in its force, from the sufferer's point of view. The outcry of Job is expressive of the common experience of the race.

The absence of the God he had known becomes the key to the dreadful emptiness in which Job finds himself. Such loneliness has little to do with the absence of others. It is the change in all things that sets a man apart in the midst of his fellows, abandoned on a terrible strand such as that suggested by Aeschylus' lines:

> And there was left the wild waves' play,
> Heard in the lone of loveless night
> On that disastrous shore.
> —*The Persians*, p. 25

His world falling apart, Job clings with terrible stubbornness to the thin thread of life and demands an answer to his problem. Anguish and loss are not the basic issues; having no choice, one endures these as bravely as he can. The suffering of Job is simply a means by which a deeper issue is brought into discussion—the honor of God and man, centered around Job's insistence on his integrity in the midst of a world gone mad.

The Job of the prologue had understood his own identity, his humanity, in the light of the existence of God. His God

50

was everywhere manifest, not so importantly in the natural world or in history generally as in man's personal and social life. God was responsible for the felicity of Job's world; he saw to it that the necessary discomforts and annoyances of human experience would be little more than that. Pain and disappointment remained decent and tolerable. Job's goodness was a creature goodness, a predictable response to favorable stimuli. Happy in himself and in his little cosmos, Job had understood that the world's misery was fundamentally self-inflicted. Ungrateful men disobeyed God and received terrible recompense.

Man really was the architect of his own well-being. God provided a vast, efficient clearinghouse by which the investments of human morality were guaranteed by inexhaustible credits. Really good men, one supposes, could from time to time glimpse through the smoke of intercessory sacrifice the bland, approving face of the infallible Teller.

There was no way for natural man to sense the existence of God other than in the categories of his own experience. So long as his own life made sense, heaven made sense. So long as he was able to ascribe the general difficulties of history to man's failure to uphold his end of the bargain, such difficulties rather supported than threatened Job's vision of himself as a creature under the wing of God.

It is the sudden, inexplicable outrage of catastrophe that dismays Job. No discernible pattern of divine moral strategy emerges. It is as though an insane God is attacking his own best soldier. The artist is shattering his fairest work. (Cf. 10:8-13.)

#### THE LOSS OF STATUS

Job's first response in the dialogue is a shuddering away of wounded flesh from the point of impact, a longing for the sweet anesthesia of death. Out of his creature outcry, however, a new identity begins to emerge: that of orphaned and alien man, forced from a new womb, naked and shivering and resentful. The birth which Job laments in chapter three is not really biological, for through his happy years he never had regretted this. He is really protesting the new birth which has impelled him from the warm safety of God-shielded living into a terrible, frightening void, fraught with unsuspected agonies, demanding outrageous effort, prophesying heartbreak and terror.

Of course Job asks to return to the warm, comfortable sanity of his old life. In restoration he intends to rediscover himself, and in himself to reassert the fundamental dignity of man. This dignity, this capacity to be one's natural self unviolated, to complete one's natural cycle and move through the triumph of fulfillment, is man's human right. For God either to commission or permit the wanton destruction of the honor of a good man is for *him* to act dishonorably.

The fundamental outrage of Job's agonies he conceives to be insult. By the same token, the object of his efforts is justification and reconciliation. This he feels will be possible if the truth about his case can be made known to God. He can then forgive God for His previous errors in policy.

In the development of his argument, Job makes certain that the hearer understands that the good life is structured about the honor of man. In the lawyer's summation with which he begins his final appeal (29-31), Job nostalgically reviews his happy years.

> Oh, that I were as in the months of old,
>     as in the days when God watched over me;
> when his lamp shone upon my head
>     and by his light I walked through darkness;
> as I was in my autumn days,
>     when the friendship of God was upon my tent;

> when the Almighty was yet with me,
>> when my children were about me;
> when my steps were washed with milk,
>> and the rock poured out for me streams of oil!
>> —29:2-6

He was held in honor by his community, enjoying the deference of the mightiest.

> When I went out to the gate of the city,
>> when I prepared my seat in the square,
> the young men saw me and withdrew,
>> and the aged rose and stood;
> the princes refrained from talking,
>> and laid their hand on their mouth.
>
> . . . . . . . . . .
>
> I chose their way, and sat as chief,
>> and I dwelt like a king among his troops,
> like one who comforts mourners.
>> —29:7-9, 29:25

Aeschylus describes the tragic hero Oedipus in similar terms:

> This was well seen in Oedipus ill-starred.
> High in the Gods' regard
> He stood; by the fireside of him was laud;
> In streets and squares where'er men walk abroad
> Or great assemblies gather in debate,
> Was never wight so praised.
> —*Seven Against Thebes*, p. 35

Job was indeed rich, but for philanthropic purposes. He had been a one-man social security department.

> I was eyes to the blind,
>> and feet to the lame.
> I was a father to the poor,

> and I searched out the cause of
> him whom I did not know.
> I broke the fangs of the unrighteous,
> And made him drop his prey from his teeth.
> —29:15-17

Such a man had every right to expect a long, happy life. Death would be discreet and not unpleasant. Like the wicked man Job bitterly describes in his response to Zophar, who

> Dies in full prosperity,
> being wholly at ease and secure,
> his body full of fat
> and the marrow of his bones moist.
> —21:23-24

the good man would happily expire, having known complete fulfillment.

Eliphaz, holding out the lure of recovery to the ailing Job, likewise emphasizes the security and safety of the good man.

> In famine he will redeem you from death,
> and in war from the power of the sword.
> . . . . . . . . . . . .
> You shall be in league with the stones of the field,
> and the beasts of the field shall
> be at peace with you.
> —5:20, 23

Similarly, old age becomes the crowning triumph of a good life.

> You shall come to your grave in a ripe old age,
> as a shock of grain comes up to
> the threshing floor in its season.
> —5:26

Of course, the good man was not perfect in the absolute sense. Job's emphasis upon his innocence refers specifically to the charge, implied in his punishment and put into words by his friends (22:5-11), that he was the worst of sinners. Surely a gentleman may defer occasionally to the weaknesses of his lower nature without being declared post-haste a criminal! God is even so unreasonable as to require of Job the sins of his youth (13:26), really no more than the mischievous cavortings of a young horse just being broken to harness.

In any event, sin is hardly the business of God. He is too big for such trivialities.

> If I sin, what do I to thee, thou
> watcher of men?
> —7:20

So far as man is concerned, sin is one's own business.

> Even if it be true that I have erred,
> my error remains with myself.
> —19:4

Job had been a gentleman of honor. He had lived in a sensible, predictable world under the care of a dependable God. A man got essentially what he deserved. Just as God might be expected to overlook a little mischief in his creatures, so might man bear without complaint the occasional bruises and disappointments of a busy, satisfying life. But what can be said for a God who flings his mightiest, most faithful noble to the dust, who exposes him to the insults of clowns and fools, who leaves him wallowing in his own blood, deadly wounded by arrows flung in unnecessary practice, abandoned and alone? Job demands that God vindicate himself by vindicating Job. To restore the honor of Job—and of the race for which Job has become spokesman—is to establish the honor of God.

FUTILITY OF HUMAN EXISTENCE

From the very beginning of the dialogue Job understands that his plight is not, after all, unique. A kind of dreadful futility overshadows the general lot of mankind. Others seek the grave, as men dig for treasure (3:20-22). Man has a hard service upon the earth; he is heaven's hired hand (7:1-2). Though apparently interminable, his life is but a breath (7:4-10).

> Man that is born of a woman
>   is of few days, and full of trouble.
> He comes forth like a flower, and withers;
>   he flees like a shadow, and continues not.
>                                   —14:1-2

Brief as are his days, their number is already determined (14:5), and those robbed from man's enjoyment are forever irreplaceable. For all his pretensions—and for that matter attainments—man cannot answer the ultimate questions (28).

The author of Ecclesiastes has insisted that while there is comparative good to be known in man's brief span of life (Eccl. 5:18), ultimately all is vanity (Eccl. 1:2). While all was well with him, Job was able to live for the day, heedless of what came after. Now that God has apparently removed his capacity to live well in the moment, he is confronted by the predicament implicit in all human life: the annihilating, indiscriminate shadow of death.

How can God fashion a human body with such care, such loving attention to detail, such actual affection (10: 7-12), knowing full well the horrible dissolution which is bound to come? The evil which is ahead is so certain that man cannot by any means avoid it. Man, being man, is in disgrace whether he be righteous or wicked.

56

If I am wicked, woe to me!
　　If I am righteous, I cannot lift up my head,
for I am filled with disgrace
　　and look upon my affliction.
　　　　　　　—10:15

Human beings are, for all they may for the moment accomplish, caricatures of God. Underneath the vestments of their pride, body and mind are surely passing away. From the moment of birth, they are stricken with the blight of mortality. This is the existential insult to which all men are subject.

Job therefore asserts that since man is by nature mortal, inept, and inconsequential, God should not lower himself to devote to such a one the mysterious purposes hidden in his Herculean wrath.

　　　Wilt thou frighten a driven leaf,
　　　　and pursue dry chaff?
　　　　　　　—13:25

"He drags me away, as if he had captured a strong man, and sees not that he is slaying a corpse, the shadow of a vapour, a mere phantom." (Sophocles *Philoctetes*, p. 190.) To shower his thunders upon such an object is for God to demean himself. Let him keep his ancient distance, grandly overseeing cosmic projects but allowing man the meager comfort of his insignificance and anonymity.

　　　What is man, that thou dost make so much of him,
　　　　and that thou dost set thy mind upon him,
　　　dost visit him every morning,
　　　　and test him every moment?
　　　　　　　—7:17-18

Yet the very violence of his denunciation of the ways of God belies Job's claim that man is a minute and valueless

57

object. Sophocles has said, "Nothing that is vast enters into the life of mortals without a curse." (*Antigone*, p. 136.) His agony is not small; the capacity to suffer greatly, to know the bitterness of high outrage, draws him from his early posture of self-deprecation to assert once again the lost dignity of man. No longer is he resigned to death and extinction.

There is unholy irony in the decay of the vigor of a strong man. Job's strength was not simply the arrogant sufficiency of the proud, but the gentle, comforting power of the compassionate. Eliphaz makes certain Job does not forget this.

> Your words have upheld him who was stumbling,
>   and you have made firm the feeble knees.
> But now it has come to you, and you are impatient;
>   it touches you, and you are dismayed.
>
> —4:4-5

Job accuses the friends of being more concerned over the disappearance of his capacity to sustain the community than over his own plight (6:19-23). "Whom can we depend on now?" they are frantically asking.

The pain Job experiences is savage and relentless.

> If I speak, my pain is not assuaged,
>   and if I forbear, how much of it leaves me?
>
> . . . . . . . . . . . . . . . .
>
> I was at ease, and he broke me asunder;
>   he seized me by the neck and dashed me to pieces.
>
> —16:6, 12

Thus, by his own confession, he has been turned into a whimpering, self-centered creature.

> He feels only the pain of his own body,
>   and he mourns only for himself.
>
> —14:22

Even though at the end of the dialogue he manages to gather his wits together in a sort of final, transcending fury, he does not let the spectator forget what an unbelievable parody of humanity he has become.

> And now my soul is poured out within me;
>> days of affliction have taken hold of me.
> The night racks my bones,
>> and the pain that gnaws me takes no rest.
> With violence it seizes my garment;
>> it binds me about like the collar of my tunic.
>> —30:16-18

Sophocles describes the agony of Heracles in similar terms: "Glued to my sides, it has eaten my flesh to the inmost parts; it is ever with me, sucking the channels of my breath; already it hath drained my fresh life-blood, and my whole body is wasted, a captive to these unutterable bonds." (*Trachinae*, p. 179.) Even here, it is the *indignity* of pain that Job especially laments.

> I go about blackened, but not by the sun;
>> I stand up in the assembly, and cry for help.
> I am a brother of jackals,
>> and a companion of ostriches.
>> —30:28-29

He has been pushed past his body's capacity to bear pain; his strength is not "the strength of stones," nor is his body bronze (6:12). As running water inexorably wears away stone, so Job's hopes, once so real, so impregnable, have eroded away before the attacks of God (14:18-21).

Job's disgrace is the unanswerable one of failing to be an authentic man. Such disgrace is seen in the babbling of senile men once wise and strong, in the obscene giggling of madwomen, in the comic lurch of cripples, the tiresome whining of beggars. The insult of Job's condition is that indefensible condition in itself! Job is like a brainwashed prisoner, a frightened, cringing animal, covered by his own ordure, whimpering before well-groomed and laughing captors. To say, "But it isn't his fault!" is both true and irrelevant. One does not argue with an odor.

In the necessary egocentricity of pain, there is a violation of man's finer nature. Himself the prisoner of tortured nerves and tissues, no longer in command of the sensitive machinery of his conscious being, he becomes another Job, pettish, self-contradictory, irrational. Eliphaz indignantly reproaches him for violating the calm objectivity necessary to contemplative discussion.

> Why does your heart carry you away,
>     and why do your eyes flash,
> that you turn your spirit against God,
>     and let such words go out of your mouth?
>                            —15:12-13

But Job had already disclaimed responsibility for what he says.

> Do you think that you can reprove words,
>     when the speech of a despairing man is wind?
>
> . . . . . . . . . . . .
>
> Let him take his rod away from me,
>     and let not dread of him terrify me.
> Then would I speak without fear of him
>     for I am not so in myself.
>                    —6:26, 9:34-35

Beyond all suffering lies the ultimate disgrace of death. Indeed Job at first seeks death; but Sheol is attractive only against the backdrop of the unendurable pain of living (3:11-22). Soon enough Job sees death to be the grim underscoring of life's futility.

As the cloud fades and vanishes,
    so he who goes down to Sheol does not come up.
                                     —7:9

Even a tree, once cut down, may sprout again from the old stump (14:7-9), but the life of man is forever extinguished in death.

As waters fail from a lake,
    and a river wastes away and dries up,
So man lies down and rises not again;
    till the heavens are no more he will not awake,
    or be roused out of his sleep.
                —14:11-12

The grave represents not only the death of the flesh, but the death of hope and dignity; Job will become the brother of the carrion worm.

If I say to the pit, "You are my father,"
    and to the worm, "My mother," or "My sister,"
where then is my hope?
    who will see my hope?
Will it go down to the bars of Sheol?
    Shall we descend together into the dust?
              —17:14-16

THE CRUSHING MAGNIFICENCE OF GOD

                    Learn to know thy heart,
And, as the times, so let thy manners change,
For by the law of change a new God rules.
But, if these bitter, savage, sharp-set words
Thou ventest, it may be, though he sit throned
Far off and high above thee, Zeus will hear;
And then thy present multitude of ills
Will seem the mild correction of a babe

.   .   .   .   .   .   .   .   .   .   .   .   .

Therefore, while thou hast me for schoolmaster,

61

> Thou shalt not kick against the pricks; the more
> That an arch-despot who no audit dreads
> Rules by his own rough will.
>> (Aeschylus *Prometheus Bound,* p. 43)

Apparently Bildad is not disturbed by the prospect of man's ultimately joining the worms. Summing up the spirit of all the friends' discourses in his last (perhaps fragmentary) speech, he concludes,

> How then can man be righteous before God?
>> How can he who is born of woman be clean?
> Behold, even the moon is not bright
>> and the stars are not clean in his sight;
> how much less man, who is a maggot,
>> and the son of man, who is a worm!
>>> —25:4-6

Bildad closes upon the note impressively sounded by Eliphaz in his report of the oracle dream.

> Can mortal man be righteous before God?
>> can a man be pure before his maker?
> Even in his servants he puts no trust,
>> and his angels he charges with error;
> how much more those who dwell in
>> houses of clay,
>> whose foundation is in the dust,
>> who are crushed before the moth.
>>> —4:17-19

Eliphaz, in his second speech, repeats essentially the same argument (15:14-16); Zophar argues similarly that the majesty of God puts him beyond appeal. In comparison with God, man is necessarily stupid and ephemeral (11: 6-12, 20:4-11). The note of necessity in human sinfulness is sounded by Aeschylus, who says,

Sin may be thrust upon us:
Evil when Heaven sends it, who shall shun?
—*Seven Against Thebes*, p. 35

While the righteousness of which Job and his friends speak is in some sense to be considered acquittal from a given charge, it also appears that man in general is considered to be essentially in the wrong before God. Angels are accused of scandal; the stars and moon are dirty in his presence! Man is categorically, inescapably unclean!

There can be, therefore, no valid complaint from any suffering person. Being a sinner, he deserves death; he is lucky to be alive. Zophar can say with perfect confidence, "Know then that God exacts of you less than your guilt deserves." (11:6c.) Ultimately, Eliphaz accuses Job of specific sins (22:5-11); presumably they explain why Job's lot is worse than that of others similarly under the curse of human nature. But God does not have to give account of his doings to man, to whose stupidity the wisdom of God would appear to be senseless caprice.

The friends therefore argue that the dishonor, the smallness, the futility of man contribute to the glory of God. It is in his presence that man's insufficiencies, by comparison, are clearly seen. Only a truly great God could reduce man's pretensions to such a shabby reality.

Eliphaz and his companions are not really pessimistic; in a way, they are optimists. There is no question but that Job may be restored. His righteousness indeed is valueless to God, who cannot be coerced by it.

Can a man be profitable to God?
Surely he who is wise is profitable to himself.
Is it any pleasure to the Almighty if you are righteous,
or is it gain to him if you make your ways blameless?
—22:2-3

However, Job's repentance will incline God's heart toward him and make possible his restoration to the ranks of all those who, their human defects grandly overlooked, live happily under divine forbearance.

The friends do not say that Job should repent of being a man. He should repent of those acts in which he went beyond necessary human error into great transgression; he must admit (whether he sees his faults clearly is apparently not too important) that he has been living a lie, and sue for mercy. (22:21-30.) But for Job to accept forgiveness under such circumstances would be further dishonor: the insult of being forgiven by one's offender.

Job readily admits the overwhelming majesty of God. He differs radically from the friends' supposition that the insignificance of man supports the divine majesty. That God's fairest work, produced with such exquisite care (10:7-12) should be reduced to miserable straits, and that by God himself, surely does not glorify him. It was easy for the contemplative Bildad to speak of man as a worm; but Job, nearest of all men to this grisly level, will not say "mother" to a maggot. (Cf. 17:14.)

He also admits the overwhelming power of God—that power which puts him beyond the reach of human coercion. But it also puts God beyond understanding human frailty. The friends insist that might makes right. Job insists that might makes wrong. One so great as God lacks the capacity to deal justly, since he is subject to no sanctions.

> Behold, he snatches away; who can hinder him?
> Who will say to him, "What doest thou?"
>
> .   .   .   .   .   .   .   .   .   .   .   .   .
>
> If it is a contest of strength, behold him!
> If it is a matter of justice, who
> can summon him?
>
> —9:12, 19

God's whim is law. So wise is he that "one could not answer him once in a thousand times" (9:2*b*). Euripides ponders the arbitrary ways of God: "Without the will of heaven none is blest, none curst, I do maintain; nor doth the same house for ever tread the paths of bliss; for one kind of fortune follows hard upon another; one man it brings to naught from his high estate, another though of no account it crowns with happiness." (*Heracleidae*, p. 253.)

He who has "marked off the heavens with a span" (Isa. 40:12*b*) towers so far above man that there can scarcely be any communication with him. Being great enough to help him, he is too remote to understand man's needs. A friendly handshake with such a giant would be a human catastrophe. In a conversation with him, Job would be so terrified and confused that, like a well-meaning bumpkin in the hands of a clever lawyer, he would become entangled in his own words, for all their artless innocence.

Job is the victim of heaven. Since God fires the poison arrows which impale him (6:4, 7:20), there can be no escape. For his helpless victim no one dare have any pity. There is no court of appeals.

> Behold, I cry out, "Violence!" but I am not answered;
> I call aloud, but there is no justice.
> —19:7

Job cannot console himself that though he is at odds with fate and his times, he is linked by his integrity to an invisible moral order which finally will be triumphant. No evidence remains of such an order. He has been flung athwart the whole stream of things.

> Have pity upon me, have pity upon me,
> O you my friends,
> for the hand of God has touched me!
> —19:21

65

### MAN'S INHUMANITY TO MAN

"No subtleties do I indulge about the powers of heaven. The faith we inherited from our fathers, old as time itself, no reasoning shall cast down; no! though it were the subtlest inventions of wits refined." (Euripides *The Bacchantes,* p. 341)

The incapacity of Job's friends to comfort him illustrates that it is man himself who carries out most cruelly and effectively what he conceives to be the just judgments of God. Having pled vainly for the boon of pity, Job bitterly cries,

> Why do you, like God, pursue me?
> Why are you not satisfied with my flesh?
> —19:22

The three friends treated him not as a person in need but as a faulty theological proposition. He exclaims, "Miserable comforters are you all!" (16:2.)

The comforters presume the role of God. Certain that they are right, these lieutenants of the majesty of heaven strut and posture, make judgments and offer terms. As Euripides wryly says, "Whoso hath the gods upon his side will have the best seer in his house." (*Helen,* p. 305.) Eliphaz believes his advice to have been the "consolations of God." (15:11)

But Job does not intend to allow the friends this complacency. He insists that in their anxiety to defend God they are partial to Him; they defend the honor of Heaven by dishonorable means.

> Will you speak falsely for God,
> and speak deceitfully for him?
> —13:7

Thus the reputation of God, Job seems to say, is in more danger from his defenders than from his attackers!

Sophocles makes something of the same point in another way. "Hateful wretch, what pleas thou canst invent! Sheltering thyself behind gods, thou makest those gods liars!" (*Philoctetes*, p. 291.) God himself will rise in anger against such sycophantic retainers.

> He will surely rebuke you
> if in secret you show partiality.
> —13:10

It is a terrible thing to bear the scorn of God. However, God in his loftiness may indeed be expected to look down on man. The real sting of insult comes when it proceeds from one's peers. The triumphant child, accompanying his mother on her mission of vengeance against the brother whose misdeed he has described, wounds with his satisfied smirk far more deeply than does the slipper applied to the seat of knowledge. Surely the thunders of God are not more to be dreaded than the happy chuckles of puritan neighbors when one's harmless amusements explode, according to pious prophecy, into catastrophe. Once a community understands that one of its citizens has clearly compromised himself before God and law, the lacerating thrust of gossip and censure pierces the already stricken brother. "Lynch the victim of God!" is often the watchword of honorable communities.

It is therefore understandable that when Job contrasts his former happiness with his present misery in his final summation (chaps. 29-30), it is his loss of social standing —his status—which receives most emphasis.

> But now they make sport of me,
> men who are younger than I,
> whose fathers I would have disdained
> to set with the dogs of my flock.
> —30:1

Here the arrogance of his pride emerges most clearly. For all the equality between master and slave which Sheol provides (3:19) and which man's common origin in the creating hands of God argues (31:13-15), there are some social outcasts who deserve no man's respect.

> They are driven out from among men;
> they shout after them as after a thief.
>
> . . . . . . . . .
>
> Among the bushes they bray;
> under the nettles they huddle together.
> —30:5, 7

Of course, Job must present such human dregs as starkly as possible, that the scandal of his case may be clear. Sub-human creatures make sport of him!

> And now I have become their song,
> I am a byword to them.
>
> . . . . . . . . . . . . . .
>
> Because God has loosed my cord and humbled me,
> they have cast off restraint in my presence.
> —30:9, 11

When the "oath of clearance" (chap. 31) is virtually completed, Job reasserts his dignity as a citizen of a world of honor. He will take the indictment of his adversary and display it for all to see.

> Surely I would carry it on my shoulder;
> I would bind it on me as a crown;
> I would give him an account of all my steps;
> like a prince I would approach him.
> —31:36-37

He refuses to accept either the stigma of his human smallness or responsibility for the extraordinary sins he is accused of committing.

The issue is clearly joined. The honor of Job as representative citizen of a moral universe has been impugned. What has happened is a violation of his nature; he is the victim of God. While the violence done to him is largely external, its real impact is within. Job is under personal attack. His only defense is his integrity. His assertion of integrity is the climax of the debate with the friends.

> Far be it from me to say that you are right;
>> till I die I will not put away my integrity from me.
> I hold fast my righteousness, and will not let it go;
>> my heart does not reproach me for any of my days.
>> —27:5-6

This same integrity is the center of the attacks made upon him both by Satan (1:9) and by the friends. As has been shown, all the torments of Job strike ultimately at his honor.

In the "oath of clearance," Job does not deny God's right to assign afflictions to dishonorable men. He continues to believe that the betrayal of moral law merits grievous punishment. What he refuses to accept is the violent disgrace of man by irresponsible forces beyond his own control.

It becomes obvious that the honor of God is at stake. God expects man to be moral and just; is God himself moral and just? Admittedly God controls the power of the created world. All the elements are his. Does he himself defer to the moral law which, by inference, he has held (in the interviews with Satan) to be unconditionally supreme in the conduct of the good man?

Job is in no position to threaten the power that creates and sustains the universe. Clearly rejected by society and ready to die, emaciated and fever-ridden, he represents no overt threat to the majesty of God. At the same time, however, he attacks God at a point which the power of all the world's armies could never reach. God is held responsible for indefensible outrage. All the excuses by which, in the past, the failures of God have been placed on human shoulders are canceled by Job's challenge. He speaks from the canon of experience. His life is so nearly over that nothing further to justify his suffering may now be expected.

God is granted one of two alternatives: either he must restore Job to prosperity or prove that Job was in the wrong. While Job once has spoken briefly of understanding his trials to be a test, the final challenge does not seem to raise that alternative. Grievous suffering is allowable only to those deserving it.

Job asks that he may get precisely what he deserves. The restoration of the old, happy order of things is conceived to be the *summum bonum* of his life.

### THE PRISON OF PROCESS

For if the hapless dead is to lie in dust and nothingness, while the slayers pay not with blood for blood, all regard for man, all fear of heaven, will vanish from the earth. (Sophocles *Electra*, p. 158.)

While Job has insisted that the processes of divine justice have miscarried in his case—and, for that matter, in the case of much of mankind—he never questions the desirability of a system of absolute retribution. He wants the moral universe to make sense.

Job's friends of course insist that history does make sense. Eliphaz says, sententiously,

> As I have seen, those who plow iniquity
> and sow trouble reap the same.
>
> —4:8

Bildad asserts,

> Does God pervert justice?
> Or does the Almighty pervert the right?

. . . . . . . . . . . . . . .

> Behold, God will not reject a blameless man,
>     nor take the hand of evildoers.
>             —8:3, 20

Injustice is speedily redressed.

> He takes the wise in their own craftiness;
>     and the schemes of the wily are
>         brought to a quick end.
>             —5:13

Just as the papyrus cannot grow without the marsh, and thus signals by its dryness that the water is gone (8:11-12), so people who are suddenly blighted witness the absence of God (8:13). The middle cycle of speeches dwells principally on the gloomy prospects of the wicked (cf. 15:16-35; 17:4-21; 20:4-29).

Job has agreed, in his attempt to remind the friends that he can quote authorities as well as they, that God works mightily in the world.

> If he tears down, none can rebuild;
>     if he shuts a man in, none can open.
>             —12:14

He conspicuously fails to say, however, that the wicked are the targets of divine chastisement. Dignity and nobility suffer God's incomprehensible wrath.

> He leads counsellors away stripped,
>     and judges he makes fools.
> He looses the bond of kings,
>     and binds a waistcloth on their loins.
> He leads priests away stripped,
>     and overthrows the mighty.
>             —12:17-19

The late speech in which Job admits the miserable fate of sinners (27:13-22) is too likely to be out of place to be considered safely representative of his views.

The friends, of course, had to admit that sometimes the wicked prosper; but their prosperity is only apparent. It is a brief interlude before catastrophe.

> Do you not know this from of old,
>   since man was placed upon earth,
> that the exulting of the wicked is short,
>   and the joy of the godless but
>     for a moment?
>         —20:4-5

The evil man will be executed by his own fiendish devices (18:7-8). He will succumb to the self-poisoning of his own malice (20:12-15), and be impoverished by his own greed (20:20-22).

The three lieutenants of God who minister to the theological needs of Job are quite certain that, whatever the appearance of things, absolute justice is being carried out. Their views are easy to hold so long as one deals only with appearances. But Job experiences evil as a reality, and he cannot accept the platitudes of the past. He will not allow himself violently to be forced into a dogmatic system protecting the honor of God while the truth of his innocence is immorally denied.

However, the system of divine retribution, in the structure of a cause-and-effect moral order, still represents the ideal of Job as well as the friends. In such a system, a man knows where he stands. He will be demoralized neither by the seductions of undeserved good fortune nor by the terrors of unmerited catastrophe. Negotiations with God can again be carried on without fear or excitement.

> Let him take his rod away from me,
>   and let not dread of him terrify me.

> Then I would speak without fear
> of him,
> for I am not so in myself.
> —9:34-35

### THE FRANTIC HYPOTHESES

The intensity of Job's sufferings and the bitter injustices he experiences lead him, paradoxically, to momentary flashes of hope which go beyond what his early comfortable days either needed or could have supported. The sense of justice which he fiercely holds along with his integrity causes him to seek solutions radical enough to reach the extremity of his lostness; such solutions are prophetic utterances of some of the highest expectations of religion.

For instance, Job's new awareness of the gap between himself and God suggests the need for an arbiter to whom both man and God might submit their complaints.

> For he is not a man, as I am, that
> I might answer him,
> that we should come to trial together.
> There is no umpire between us,
> who might lay his hand upon us both.
> —9:32-33

It might be objected that such an umpire, by exercising authority over God, would be apparently superior to God himself. But Job is speaking the language of need, the need for at least a mediary between the God who in his greatness is inaccessible to man and the man to whom he is nevertheless indispensable.

Indeed, if God removes from Job the anguish which makes it impossible for him to speak soberly and rationally (cf. Eliphaz' rebuke, 4:5; 5:1-2), he will also remove the impulse which raises the questions to be discussed. Religious questions may be argued without heat and in sweet

73

reasonableness so long as the issues are not vital. When the clash of convictions scissors close to the jugular, passion shapes the vocabulary of faith.

Job does not really believe there can be an arbiter between the claims of God and man. One was not needed in the old family-reunion days. Nothing in the retribution dogma of Sunday-school homilies supported such a possibility. Only the language of perplexity and despair sprung from the experience of outrage reveals that there is *not* an umpire! Behind this negation is a positive assertion: there *ought* to be one! Just as Job in his temporal frailty cannot play the role of an imperturbable god (cf. 6:11-13), it is equally absurd for God to play the role of a capricious or resentful man.

> Hast thou eyes of flesh?
> Dost thou see as man sees?
> Are thy days as the days of man,
>   or thy years as man's years,
> that thou dost seek out my iniquity
> And search for my sin,
> although thou knowest that I am
>     not guilty,
>   and there is none to deliver out
>   of thy hand?
> —10:4-7

Someone—someone extraordinary—is needed to bring together in one mind, in one category of demand and responsibility, alienated man and transcendent God.

What kind of being can do this? Job does not say. In the evocative force of such a passage, it is perhaps impossible for anyone to avoid reading in his own prejudices. Nor perhaps should he try to avoid so doing. It is a function of such a work as Job, after all, to confront man in a new way with ideas already his own. To me, Job's in-

74

credible umpire is clearly distinct from any known category. What kind of person might he be? Neither god or man? Both god and man? A god who is sympathetic to man? A human acceptable to God? A new deity who subsumes the inadequacies of both God and man under a new order of justice? If the last hypothesis is correct—which is far from unreasonable—should not Job be addressing his claim to the *umpire* rather than to the opponent who fouls him so outrageously?

Basically, the absence of the arbiter is used by Job to increase the pathos of his case, so that his opponent might withdraw his punishing hand. The improbable has been stated, however; in its sudden daring, it strangely articulates that need for priest and mediator which is almost universal in religion. Strange it is indeed that behind the ministries of priests and prelates, there may have been the cry of the rebel, expressive of man's dissatisfaction with the ways of God.

Another hope that sprang from Job's despair was for an afterlife. The old Sheol doctrine suited well enough, perhaps, for the man who anticipated a full life and could see his own personality incarnate in the flesh of his children. Moreover, in the first shock of outrage any change might be preferred; at least Sheol would not perpetuate present anguish.

Now, however, Job's children are dead. His own life is being cut off before fulfillment. His sense of the injustice of his treatment, intensified by the debate into outrage, overwhelms his pain. Where once he begs for death (3:20-23), he now begs for life. His present life will not be restored. He is not like a tree, capable of regenerating life from the rotten stump of a dead body.

> So man lies down and rises not again;
> till the heavens are no more he

will not awake,
or be roused out of his sleep.
—14:12

Bonds He may loose, for durance find a balm,
And work, howso He please, deliverance.
But when the dust hath drunk the blood of man
And he's once dead, there's no uprising; spell
For that my Father hath created not.
—Aeschylus *Euminides*, p. 88

Nothing in the conventional retributive pattern held in common by Job and his companions either demanded or could give a basis for a restoration of life after death. Job's reference to the sprouting of a dead tree stump (14:7-9) was the desperate grasping of an exception. By and large, the harvest time of life, symbolized by the reverend white hairs of age, had been a fitting climax to the human story. As spokesman for this view, Eliphaz says,

You shall come to your grave in ripe old age,
as a shock of grain comes up to
the threshing floor in its season.
—5:26

It is one thing for death to be the quiet, expected termination of a fulfilled life. It is quite another for one to be cut down before the "full grain" is in the ear. Death is no longer a granary but a prison. Job's outcry, "If a man die, shall he live again?" reaches beyond Sheol, groping for a restoration of his identity so that he can complete life's unfinished business.

Job does not ask for resurrection as compensation for what he has suffered. So radical is his request that nothing in human experience could conceivably merit it. He is not seeking simply for release from pain, as he once had done. He does not attribute to the restored life the delights of paradise, nor does he stipulate the return of any of his forfeited possessions.

Job asks for life, real life, substantial life beyond death as a means of reconciliation to God. He is willing to be hidden in Sheol for ages if there may be a termination at last, in the slow cooling of the wrath of God, of the unendurable alienation which he now knows.

> O that thou wouldest hide me in Sheol,
>> that thou wouldest conceal me
>> until thy wrath would be past,
>> that thou wouldest appoint me a
>> set time, and remember me!
> If a man die, shall he live again?
>> All the days of my service I would wait,
>> till my release should come.
> Thou wouldest call, and I would answer thee;
> Thou wouldest long for the work of thy hands.
>
> —14:13-15

Again God would watch over him and his sins would be forever forgotten (14:16-17).

Here as before, the hopes of Job are lifted only to be abandoned. He proceeds to lament the slow erosion of human aspirations; as "the waters wear away the stones . . . so thou destroyest the hope of man" (14:19a, c). Indeed, Job has a *rhetorical* purpose under the didactic force of his utterances. He will be satisfied simply to speak again with God. Why then, one supposes, should God refuse to speak to him now?

Nonetheless, this passage illustrates a fundamental truth: that life after death becomes a doctrine of spiritual significance, not as an end in itself, but as an indispensable precondition to personal reconciliation with God. The paraphernalia of heaven, however man chooses to under-

77

stand it, can neither be deserved by human merit nor can it compensate for history's injustices. The golden streets are symbolic of a fellowship transcending surroundings; the heavenly banquet represents a supper beyond food.

Job looks to heaven for the restoration of human dignity. At the same time that he asks for the enforcement of a system of justice and order such as he supposed existed in his untroubled years, he is compelled to ask for something further that the past had not demanded. Thus the agony of Job again provides new dimensions for the sufficiency of God.

Job's emotional movement from despair to rebellion is never more clear than when he cries,

> O earth, cover not my blood,
> and let my cry find no resting place.
> —16:18

Ancients used to believe that blood which soaked into the ground was silent, but that if it gathered upon a rock it called forever for vengeance. With no evidence that God would remember him through the interminable eons of Sheol, Job harks back to the superstitious beliefs of his fathers. Somehow, slaughtered innocence will receive redress; the blood of Abel will still call to God (Gen. 4:10).

Immediately after this outcry, Job expresses a startling confidence:

> Even now, behold, my witness is in heaven,
> and he that vouches for me is on high.
> —16:19

Eliphaz has sternly cautioned Job against attempting to rely upon angelic interventions.

Call now; is there any one who will answer you?
To which of the holy ones will you turn?
—5:1

Job and his friends have agreed that God is hostile to him.
Who is the witness in heaven?

The divine witness is either God himself or some other
supernatural being separate from God. Since Job has insisted all the way through the dialogue that God is not on
his side, and since in the earlier part of the same chapter
he has spoken bitterly of himself as the victim of God
(16:6-17), it seems incredible that he should suddenly—
and momentarily—reverse his whole point. It seems much
easier to suppose that Job believed that an intercessory
angel or divine being of some sort was taking his side.

Certainly no evidence can be adduced to prove the
existence of such a powerful ally. Job reaches his position
on the basis of what, according to moral law, *must* be.
There has to be a rescue for the righteous. Somewhere and
in some way, somebody cares. The purpose of this hidden
friend is to guarantee the social and spiritual rights of men.

That he would maintain the right
of a man with God,
like that of a man with his neighbor.
—16:21

The obscurity of Job 16:17-21, partly due to textual
difficulties, makes it undesirable to lean heavily upon the
passage as evidence of Job's belief in a heavenly inter-
cessor. A longer, though still difficult, passage subsequently
seems to corroborate the idea, however.

Job has just finished his account of his abandonment by
the whole human community (19:13-20); he has vainly
implored the friends for pity (19:21-22). Then he breaks
forth:

> Oh that my words were written!
>    Oh that they were inscribed in a book!
> Oh that with an iron pen and lead
>    they were graven in the rock forever!
> For I know that my Redeemer lives,
>    and at last he will stand upon the earth;
> and after my skin has been thus destroyed,
>    then without my flesh I shall see God,
> whom I shall see on my side,
>    and my eyes shall behold, and
>       not another.
>             —19:23-28

Such is the obscurity of this passage in Hebrew that extreme caution needs to be used in drawing conclusions from it. Nevertheless, some generalizations are possible.

The contrast between this passage and the introductory diatribe against his companions (19:13-22) indicates that the Redeemer is *the* friend. Job's disillusionment with all his friends suggests that here is a supernatural Friend, very probably the ally of chapter sixteen. The word "redeemer" means in Hebrew the next of kin, whose duty it is to avenge the blood of a brother or care for his title to property (keeping it in the family) after his death. Hardly a merciful figure, the redeemer brings justice to his own, to whom he is bound by ties of blood. As described, he is certainly not the Jewish Messiah, whose career is always bound up with the destiny of Israel.

It is not even certain whether the vindication of Job shall come before or after his death; the arbitrary "without my flesh" of 19:26b could read "from my flesh." There his been no evidence that Job's abandonment of the hope of life after death has been modified. The threat of the sword, directed toward the friends and obviously to be carried out by the Redeemer, sounds more immediate than Job's hope of a resurrection would probably be.

The real force of this passage has generally been missed. The Christian tendency to see in the redeemer of Job the figure of Christ overlooks the function of the whole passage. Fundamentally, 19:23-29 is a threat. Job's words have been disregarded or mishandled by men; God has not heard him. He wishes his case to be preserved. The Redeemer will either stand beside Job or cause God to stand beside him, and those who misinterpret Job's case will be punished. The friends themselves must then be afraid, "for wrath brings the punishment of the sword." The "judgment" mentioned in 19:29c is undoubtedly temporal and the work of that same sword.

Now it can more readily be understood why the hopes of Job drop so readily out of his conversation. He seems to soar to heights of insight and then to drop inexplicably back to where he was before. He does not "go into orbit." The reason probably is that all the passages of extraordinary hope cited are intended by Job to strengthen his case. The absence of the umpire and the impossibility of life after death show the helplessness of Job before God. In the ninetieth psalm the psalmist similarly celebrates the eternality of God in order to secure his condescension upon insignificant man (90:1-4, 13). The passages speaking of the heavenly Witness or Redeemer, on the other hand, are Job's insistence to the friends that he is not alone and that his claims for justice will eventually come to court. Once he has made his point, he drops the tools desperately contrived to make it.

In short, the demands of absolute justice, not met by any known agency, *must* be met. Such demands bring Job to hopes which are in themselves untenable, but such hopes as possess at least a momentary logic for him and promise to give him some vestige of status in the eyes of the friends.

Perhaps the most significant of all Job's statements of

hope is his assertion that once he could really get God's ear, he would be acquitted. Job would learn from God; God would listen to Job.

> I would lay my case before him
>     and fill my mouth with arguments.
> I would learn what he would answer me,
>     and understand what he would say to me.
>                                   —23:4-5

God would not, as Job had feared, confuse him and render him speechless.

> Would he contend with me in the
>     greatness of his power?
>   No; he would give heed to me.
> There an upright man could reason with him.
>     and I should be acquitted for ever by my judge.
>                                   —23:6-7

But Job cannot find the way to the heavenly seat (23:3). He is still terrified by the presence of God—the strange, unfamiliar God of arbitrary and immovable judgments (23:13-17).

Whence does Job get this apparently new confidence? It may be that faith in an arbiter of some sort has grown to the place where Job thinks he can get a fair hearing in the courts. A fair hearing is all he claims to want. However, he makes no mention here of such an arbiter.

Is it significant that Job, toward the end of the dialogue, has just begun to reflect on the *general* injustices found in the world? On one hand, one might suppose that this would be discouraging. Many wicked prosper (21:7-24) and the righteous suffer (21:25-26). How can Job hope to reverse this trend? On the other hand, Job may feel that his case is strengthened; his own testimony, attacked by the friends, is no longer necessary. God's justice is therefore impugned in the general history of mankind. Subsequently, Job dwells with great eloquence on the outrages perpetrated by man upon his fellows; this indicates that Job now rests his case significantly outside himself—on precedents brought in from common experience.

Perhaps Job has at last found human companionship. The plundered, the persecuted, the ravished are everywhere in the world. They are his brothers. He is their self-appointed spokesman at the judgment bar. It is a pleasing thing to obtain satisfaction for one's own grievance while pleading for that of another. However, Job did not seek to remonstrate with God regarding victimized mankind until he himself became a victim.

Even in the passage cited from chapter 23, Job's confidence is conditional: "If I could get a hearing! If I could find the court!" This, however, he is unable to do. So he remains terrified at the presence of God (23:15-17).

In summary, one fundamental preoccupation emerges from all that Job says. It is his obsession with justice. This depends upon two corroborating convictions: *he* has been just, but he has been unjustly treated. His highest hopes are to arrange a confrontation of God that will allow the truth to emerge and form the blueprint for his restoration. Job does not ask for the return of creature comforts for their own sake. While he certainly desires the cessation of suffering and the restoration of the good days of yore, he asks for the first as a precondition to the kind of conversation between himself and God which would make reconciliation possible, and the second as the kind of climate in which reconciliation might be experienced.

Since the Book of Job abounds in psychological overtones, a caution must be inserted here. Is Job simply a good psychologist, approaching God for consideration in ways flattering to him? Many a courtier threatened by banishment from the presence of a king has protested that he cannot live without the blessing of the king's countenance. Both the king and the courtier may be thinking of the royal smile in terms of ten silver talents a year.

When King Hezekiah congratulated the Lord that it had been in the interests of heaven for him to be healed, since fifteen more years of royal devotions would ascend on high (cf. Isa. 38:16-19), it surely did not miss the attention of God that Hezekiah could do a bit of fishing and polish off a substantial amount of apple (or fig) pie in that length of time. A cynic might well observe that Job was simply polishing the apple; he cared little about reconciliation as such, but he cared much about the emoluments that go with it.

As a suffering creature, Job whimpers for relief from distress; however, his disclaimers of responsibility due to fever, his tendency to hyperbole and exaggeration, at the same time have argumentative force. When he describes his condition, he does so with a careful eye to building an impregnable case. His noblest utterances are all overlaid with the stigma of his self-interest, his passion for vindication.

A cynical mind might, however, miss seeing in Job the expression of man's spiritual yearning. Man has never really been satisfied with bread alone. He has insisted on asking why he is here, and what purpose produced him, and to what end. The intensely rational "live-for-the-day" conclusion of Koheleth, the tired cynic of Ecclesiastes, appeals to contemplative minds but it does not satisfy the soul. However he lives, man endlessly seeks a frame of reference in which he cannot bear himself except as a spiritual identity.

The mingling of the here-and-now with the there-and-then, the conflation of spiritual and physical, is intrinsic to the experience of man. Man does not live by bread alone,

84

but he does not live without bread, either. We do not have a family reunion to eat, but we hardly have a family reunion without eating. In the Hebrew view, the breath of God was a part of being, but so was the body (Gen. 2:7).

For Job to ask God to remove the curse from his body so that he could talk to him no doubt represented a mingling of motives. In one sense what Job said was visceral: the noises of any kind of organism under stress, in this instance peculiarly articulate. In another sense what he said was spiritual: the phrasing of man's constant thrust into the maddening mystery behind his existence. Inasmuch as both these forces operate in Job, he is intensely human, speaking to and for the race.

The understanding of the pathos of Job as a legal and moral force helps to explain the tone of God's speech. God himself is on trial, not Job! Job's trial, in his own mind, has been thrown out of court and a mistrial called.

The final summons to God shows clearly how Job, resting upon the certainty of his own integrity, has resolutely drawn up his case. Far from weakening under the crossfire of the friends and the debilitation of his disease, he has gained strength, The pathos of the first cycle, the outrage of the second, and the broad survey of the third are united in a display of forensic force. Having silenced the friends, he is now prepared, like Jacob of old, to sit on the chest of God. Like the obstreperous bug of Walt Kelly's *Pogo,* who shouts to a startled alligator in the house, "Step outside and say that!" Job challenges God to strip off the paraphernalia of his power and meet him upon the field of moral truth.

Are we not then too proud, when heaven hath made such preparation for our life, not to be content therewith? But our presumption seeks to lord it over heaven, and in the pride of our hearts we think we are wiser than the gods. . . . For the

85

deity, confusing their destinies, doth oft destroy by the sinner's fate him who never sinned nor committed injustice.

—Euripides *The Suppliants,* p. 260

Should God not appear, Job will be the victor in that aspect of power that Satan sensed clearly enough in his first analysis. Just as man is presumed to be moral only because he prizes the safety of the fence of God, so God remains God only because he can throw ramparts around heaven. Should God's hands be tied his superiority would be reduced to that found only in the bombast of earthquake, wind, and fire. "Whosoever of mortal men transgresses, him the gods punish. How, then, can it be just that you should enact your laws for men, and yourselves incur the charge of breaking them?" (Euripides *Ion,* p. 286.)

On the other hand, should God appear Job is certain that he will be vindicated. God will then be forced to restore Job and repair the world whose disorder Job has cited. In this process God must admit he has been in the wrong. Moreover, should God appear, would it not seem that he has had to interfere with the freedom of the original experiment, manipulating the data so it will come out his way, so there might be no administrative embarrassment to upset the agenda of the heavenly council?

At long last God is himself caught in the *either-or* that has given man his worst moments. Euripides puts it, "Either thou art a god of little sense, or else naturally unjust." (*Heracles Mad,* p. 368.) Again and again Everyman had found himself trapped in the unyielding arms of moral law.

That the noble code of chapter 31 is predominantly moral, appealing to the conscience and highlighting the inner man, increases the predicament of God. Job does not make the mistake of asserting a formal piety, citing his prayers and sacrifices. God might easily insist that such works were inconclusive. Job emphasizes above all his concern for the welfare of others. He would not assault the honor of his neighbor's wife (31:1-2), despise the cause of his servant (31:13-15), or neglect the needs of the poor (31:16-21). He would not set his mind upon money or secretly worship the sun and moon (31:24-27). He has not been hypocritical nor fearful of human censure (31:33-34). He has dealt faithfully with his land (31:38-39). In short, Job has been the faithful overseer of *his* universe. He has pruned and dressed his garden; why should he be cast out of paradise?

The good deeds Job celebrates in his summation are the sort that proceed from honor. He looks honorably at maidens (31:1) and is not enticed by his neighbor's wife (31:9). He sustains the worth of slaves (31:13) and cares for the helpless (31:16-31). Secure within his own faith, he does not seek reassurance from wealth or the sun and moon (31:24-28). He has not rejoiced in the ruin of enemies (31:29) or allowed fear of censure to force him into hypocrisy (31:33-34). The goodness of Job has not been required by statute; it is the expression of *honor!*

As a man of honor, Job approaches God as a prince rather than a worm (31:37). As a man of honor he demands no more nor less than honorable treatment and a fair trial before law.

Job's challenge clearly asserts that God has not dealt faithfully with *his* world as Job has done with his. Job would not have allowed injustice to a good man. He who took interest in helpless wayfarers would not have put a faithful retainer to torture. He who cared little for gold would not have allowed the delights of celestial gardens to distract his mind from the needs of his servants. He who never concealed his own guilt when he was in the wrong would never have declared a man guilty without stating the charges.

From the standpoint of phenomenal power, God is on his throne; he is in no jeopardy. But from the standpoint of the immovable, transcendant realities of right and wrong, apart from which his power most ultimately must be declared demonic, heaven is under attack. A promethean giant is beating at the ramparts with a force such as one third of heaven and the black Napoleon of the primeval fire-fight never mustered.

For Job has discovered that he really is God. In human history, this discovery is by no means new; it first occurred in Eden. Subsequently, the whole race has paused at the forbidden tree, seeking a shortcut to divinity. That Job takes the seat of majesty should not surprise us, for by now we surely know who Job is.

Job is mankind.

# V

# God's Speech: From the Storm's Center

The position of Elihu's speech poses a structural problem in treating the Book of Job. Whatever theory is held as to either the composition or content of these materials, there is no question but that Elihu functions as a sort of bridge between Job's challenge and God's response. Such a bridge connects two points; it can best be examined in light of the relationship of the two. It is therefore advisable at this point to postpone the Elihu materials and examine God's speech.

The alternatives before Job, from the standpoint of the prologue, were either to curse or not to curse God. In the first account of Job's response to the test, he blessed God. In the poetry, however, he does neither. He leaves the situation unresolved until he receives the information on the purposes of God that he deems is necessary before he takes a final stance.

Strictly from the point of view of the prologue, God cannot come to Job without a moral violation of the terms of the test. It is difficult to tell how far the author of the poetry felt compelled to remain true to these terms, but it seems likely to me that they laid some constraint upon the speech.

It is, however, probable that the strangely noncommital nature of the voice from the storm is due more to the necessity that God, to be God, remain mystery than that he be true to the original terms of the experiment. Both Job and the friends have *played* God. It is up to God first of all to *be* God. So to be means, among other things, that God not commit himself to nostrums and doctrines which, while they medicate and explain, are always in competition with other medications and explanations. Like a king for whose immediate policies underlings must take responsibility so that the proper public image of the tyrant may be preserved, God does not enter directly into the argument regarding his justice to man.

God's speech does not really violate the principle of his absence from Job. Intimate, personal conversation is not carried out by the medium of storms, with the howl of tornados and the peremptory cannonade of thunder. If anything, the phenomenal distance between God and man is increased.

> Who is this that darkens counsel
> by words without knowledge?
> Gird up your loins like a man,
> I will question you, and you shall
> declare to me.
> Where were you when I laid the
> foundation of the earth?
> Tell me, if you have understanding.
>
> —38:2-4

The whole speech reveals nothing of God's care for man, of the possibility of restoration, of hidden purposes working through human trials. Most of it is, from the stand-point of logical debate, a sublime irrelevance. Were one to wipe out the questions, elaborately adorned with information Job already knows, were one to eliminate the ostrich, fabulous Behemoth, and Leviathan, there would remain scarcely more than the chiming of incredible music and an inarticulate shouting.

### BEYOND PROCESS

God does not meet Job on his own terms; he has not chosen either of the alternatives Job thoughtfully supplied to him. He speaks past the dilemma presented to him. Job and the friends had failed to see that, so far as God's relations with man are concerned, for God simply to guarantee to man the proper result of his every action would be to reduce himself to moral insignificance. He would become a personal neuter. An infinite IBM machine, he would never be free to act on his own.

Such a God is helpless before either human vice or human virtue. A good bureaucrat could just as well work out the facts and assign the rain or the locusts; all God would really have to do is supply the muscle. Now man can live intelligently. He can figure out what he wants and make the moves necessary to get it. God is great and just; all a just man wants from him is a guarantee that the system will work; otherwise, the scandalous possibility arises that man may not get what comes to him.

People discover a kind of moral law operative in history. Men frequently become their own executioners. Wealthy people are often reduced to rags, and thrifty people become wealthy. Pious people stubbornly persist and the meek inherit the earth. Those who sow hatred reap death. One can even persuade himself he has not seen "the righteous forsaken or his children begging bread" (Ps. 37:25). Any historian knows that, all other conditions being equal, frugal, moral, conscientious, and hardworking people are the world's best citizens and taxpayers.

All human experience rests upon the structure of cause and effect. The simplest actions—tying a shoe, peeling potatoes, sharpening the mower—are done so shoes may stay on, potatoes may be eaten, grass may be mowed. Seed is planted and sheep are sheared, roads are built and teeth filled, because man lives in confidence that expected results will follow. When they do not, most people can either discover what went wrong, so that the *system* is not jeopardized, or assume that something did, to the same effect.

Satan had suspected that Job served God only because of the predictable, dependable relationship between piety and prosperity. The rational nature of man only refines and makes more effective his creature absorption in self. Give an animal two choices, and he will choose the better for him. He will make his nest in the best branch of the tree, find the dryest spot during a rain, seek the coolest waters in the heat of summer. This is the role created things play; this is also the role Job wants permission to play. As a creature, he does not wish, having dug wells, to get brine; having paid his debts, to be cheated; having sustained others, to be victimized; and having sown barley, to reap cockle.

Just as a wild thing best attains its glory in the proper soil and climate, man develops honor in the environment of health and well-being. Job asks God to put back the torn-down fences of His care, so that in domestic safety, in the contrived greenhouse of providential oversight, Job may fulfill in good living the happiness proper to his nature.

The fence that kept Job perfectly safe, however, was in reverse function a prison: the prison of inexorable process. The cell was comfortable; the food was good. Lighting and ventilation were superior and recreation beyond criticism.

But beneath velvet was unyielding steel. Behind soft drapery was mortised granite. Man was a part of the ceaseless round of things, his history akin to the downward rushing of waters and the flawless precision of constellations.

The Job who had kept his cell tidy could hardly be expected to serve God for nothing. Good behavior brought concessions. You knew where you stood with the warden. Caged beasts, say some, are not to be pitied, for they never had it so good; pacing before bars is instinctive, comfortable exercise. Many released animals seek their cages again, as the Israelites longed for the chains and garlic of Egypt. So Job asks to go back to the elaborate, walled garden of his good days, where a man could depend on God.

Similarly, a psalmist cried for the glorious past, when God really moved for his people.

> My God, my God, why hast thou forsaken me?
> Why art thou so far from helping
> me, from the words of my groaning?
> . . . . . . . . . . . . .
> In thee our fathers trusted;
> they trusted, and thou didst deliver them.
> To thee they cried, and were saved;
> in thee they trusted, and were
> not disappointed.
> But I am a worm, and no man.
> —Ps. 22:1, 4-6

All men look back to paradise which, though in the past, really swings round to the future as ultimate goal. Elaborate attempts to reproduce this lost environment are forever being frustrated, for Adam still fears the Presence which alone is indispensable to Eden. The flaming swords at the gate are forever reminders that entrance to paradise is not behind, but ahead. The Creator who did not at once demand the dread forfeit of disobedience can now be reached only across the bridge of history, by sweat and disappointment, thorns and briars, by protesting life emerging from the outrageous struggle of human parturition (cf. Gen. 3).

The psalmist cited above illustrates Job's mood. Since men of old received direct help from God, they were better than he. He is "a worm, and no man," scorned and despised by people (Ps. 22:6). Without human dignity, he has been robbed of honor. Ultimately, however, his restoration contributes to the glory of God.

> From thee comes my praise in the great congregation;
> my vows I will pay before those who fear him.
> —Ps. 22:25

Similarly, Job asks for a restoration of the old *status quo*. Accepting the role of a hireling, he wants his wages. A created thing, he wants his nest. A moral man, he wants his honor.

The author of the book of Hebrews, arguing for the superiority of Christ over Moses as prophet, says: "Yet Jesus has been counted worthy of as much more glory than Moses as the builder of a house has more honor than the house. . . . Now Moses was faithful in all God's house as a servant, to testify to the things that were to be spoken later, but Christ was faithful over God's house as a son." (Heb. 3:3, 5-6.) The apostle Paul, arguing that the church is free from the Law of Moses, compares the church and Israel to Isaac and Ishmael; one is free and the other is slave. He cites Genesis: "Cast out the slave and her son, for the son of the slave shall not inherit with the son of the free woman." (Gal. 4:30.)

The question that must be asked of God's appearance is this: Is the voice from the whirlwind simply a noisy scolding which Job must endure before being restored to his lost estate? Is the status for which Job asks the ultimate one for man? Or can God, speaking past the necessary censorship of dramatic and theological necessity, communicate to Job that there is an honor rooted not in affluence and fame but in a constant human worth transcending circumstance? That he has a garden for other than vegetables? That there is a road ahead to a different paradise?

## THE CONFRONTATION

There are those who think that Job's answer was the confrontation itself. Before very God all conditioned questions disappear. *He is* the answer in his mysterious power and presence. Even parched lips and dry throats break into song, and glazed eyes burn with ecstasy. The friends had been talking about God; this *is* God. Beyond conversation, beyond argument, he answers the needs of men by sweeping them into himself. The body of man is flung supine, his heart captured, his helpless litany of praise begun as surely as the flower swings blindly toward the sun.

So Job, who had earlier uttered premonitions of his enthrallment and dumb terror before the austere majesty of God (cf. chap. 9), concludes:

> I had heard of thee by the hearing of the ear,
> but now my eye sees thee;
> therefore I despise myself,
> and repent in dust and ashes.
> —42:5-6

Similarly Philoctetes, at the end of his struggles, says at the appearance of the deified Heracles: "Ah, thou whose accents I had yearned to hear, thou whose form is seen after many days, I will not disobey thy words!" (Sophocles *Philoctetes*, p. 195.) It is improbable that Job actually *saw*

God in the cloud; what he doubtless means here is that he has perceived God in a new way—a real way. His knowledge of the Divine has been moved from rumor to experience.

Some think that the sin which Job admits is precisely what Eliphaz described when he insisted that before the grandeur of God man is categorically unrighteous (4:17-19). Unable to see his sin because of the defects of his own perceptions, Job suddenly senses, as Isaiah did before the glory of the celestial vision (Isa. 6:1-5), that he is inexcusably unclean. The vision of God and a sense of sin become simultaneous.

Job does not, however, repent of his pretrial days. He repents of what he has said during the trial. The last two lines of his recantation, cited above, are of uncertain translation. It is quite possible to read,

> Therefore though I am melting away,
> I am comforted in regard to dust and ashes.
> —42:6

In any event, the "abhor myself" of the R.S.V. rests on too uncertain a foundation to use as decisive evidence for Job's real point of view.

There is no doubt real merit in the idea that Job finds his answer in his "encounter" with God. God is somehow more than he had expected. His questions are neither answered nor refused; they are transcended. Job has indeed found a new status rooted in God.

The question is: What *is* this confrontation? Here one must be reminded that the poetry of Job is a work of art. The allusions of God are verbal. He speaks; he is a part of the great dialogue. Consequently the appearance of God is mediated in conversation. Otherwise a mere reference to his arrival and to Job's response would suffice to close the story. It is therefore proper to seek in the enigmatic words of God a hint of *his* conception of the ultimate status of man.

## MAN'S HONOR IN THE UNIVERSE

It has been pointed out that God's challenge to Job to "gird up his loins like a man" (40:7) and answer him preserved the distance between man and God. This is only partially true. In comparison to intuition, a conversation implies distance. The distance, however, is of another kind. Something spoken can be misunderstood, argued with, disobeyed. The forces and drives of the natural world, as they witness to God, are beyond negotiation. The categories of obedience or disobedience are irrelevant. Lightning strikes where invisible forces impel it; the sea rests in its basins and carves its shores as fast as rocks may be hewn with water. Ravens cry dissonantly for food, the ostrich remains stupidly silent, the horse shrills at the sound of the battle trumpet.

> As a horse
> All fire and fierceness pants upon the bit,
> What time, hard-held, he paweth in his place
> Mad for the sound of trumpet.
> —Aeschylus *Seven Against Thebes,* p. 31

But only man may *speak* with God. Only man is endowed with the capacity to miss the meaning of God; he only is stupid enough, helpless enough, to have to be told.

The apparent harshness of God's opening statement is in reality a compliment to Job. In being asked the response to a question, he is really being granted responsibility. Job has called to God in his aloneness; his human identity, though the dramatic context is at times ironical (38:21), is respected.

97

It is indeed true that in all God's speech there is no reference to the tragedy of Job, no expression of sympathy, no commendation for such victories as the early Job, at least, achieved. The questions God asks relentlessly press the point of man's ignorance and powerlessness.

> Where were you when I laid the
>     foundation of the earth?
> Tell me, if you have understanding.
>   .   .   .   .   .   .   .   .   .   .   .   .
> Have you commanded the morning
>     since your days began,
>     and caused the dawn to know its place?
>   .   .   .   .   .   .   .   .   .   .   .   .
> Can you bind the chains of the Pleiades,
>     or loose the cords of Orion?
>                                     —38:4, 12, 31

The whole phenomenal universe, in its creation and subsistence, is a mystery to Job. But he can consider it! He can hear the questions, and because he can hear them he can pursue them!

The questions of the voice of thunder are, in reality, the questions of science. God does not forbid investigation. He does, however, proclaim human ignorance; and it is assumed that whatever man learns, there will still be the beyond that he does not know. Job may not know "when the mountain goats bring forth" (39:1), but some snooping naturalist with binoculars is going to find out. Job may not know the ordinances of the heavens, but astronomers shall presume that they know what God is doing, so that they can prescribe his activities as surely as they can chart the skies or measure the gestation time of wild goats.

The author of the Job speeches would be amazed, no doubt, to know what man now has ascertained about the measurements of the earth (38:5), how he has now walked

the recesses of the deep (38:16), cleft channels for tor-
rents of rain (38:25),

> To bring rain on a land where no man is,
>     on the desert in which there is no man;
> to satisfy the waste and desolate land,
>     and to make the ground put forth grass.
>                                         —38:26-27

In the taming of electricity, man has in a sense sent forth
lightnings, "that they may go and say to you, 'Here we
are!' " (38:35). With cloud-seeding planes, he has even
been able to "tilt the waterskins of the heavens" (38:37*b*).
The hawk still soars in his enigmatic wisdom; but man
now outsoars the most ambitious bird. Eagles spot their
prey miles away, but man can probe through miles of
sea and thousands of miles of space for his.

Modern science would appear to have taken the thunder
out of the voice of the whirlwind. Even the chains of the
Pleiades, in a sense of the word, seem about to be un-
locked by irreverent space travelers. Armed with a couple
of modern textbooks, Job could now give a good many
answers to God's questions; presumably God, chagrined,
would have to say, "You do know quite a bit, after all," or
"Nothing that they propose to do will now be impossible
for them" (11:6).

A second thought about God's speech, however, should
make it clear that he spoke, not in relation to ultimate
problems, but from just ahead of the moving edge of
man's learning. God has always chosen to reveal himself
to man in categories he could understand. Had God asked
questions of a Greek philosopher, or a Hindu seer of the
same period, they would no doubt have been different.
The voice from the whirlwind is the revelation of wonderful, fearful mystery juxtaposed to the probings of man.

Whatever the author of Job thought the storm was saying to his hero, the questions posed clearly testify to the rise of the scientific spirit. It is of interest that this new force was placed subsequent to Job's experience of new theological freedom. The finalities of dogma can shut off from the ear of man not only fresh news of God but also new understandings of himself and his surroundings.

The voice of the storm is to be heard whenever inquirers in any of the sciences sense a Something beyond their probing and are forced back—for the moment at least—into the reverent silence of those who confront the unanswerable. Once again, the scientist finds himself confounded, jaw dropping, scratching his head, bemused like a savage with a new bauble. Hearkening to premonitory thunder beyond horizons visible, he supposes and conjectures. Ninety-nine of his solutions may be wilder than anything proposed in Grimm's fairy tales, but one may ultimately be right.

The man standing silenced before the enlarged perimeter of his ignorance, confronting the *more* that he does not know, is not humiliated before heaven. He is honored with the status of co-worker with God. He is no well-oiled robot, at one with the clicking machinery of a mechanical providence. His bewilderment is the pledge of his freedom. The mystery before him leaves room for hypothesis; hypothesis, born of curiosity and frustration, leaps into new areas of knowledge and power.

It is significant that while God speaks of his care for all creation, inanimate, animate, and fabulous, he never speaks of his care for man. The inborn self-sufficiency of creatures, by which in the power of the God of providence they care for themselves, is not attributed to the human race.

Perhaps this simply means that Job, already knowing how God cares for the rest of the world, is expected to discover for himself that providence extends to him, too.

Job has insisted that he has been important, both from the standpoint of man and God (cf. chaps. 10, 29); he knows that God cares for small things such as grass and baby ravens (38:27; 41). Should not such a God care for him, too? Can Job, speaking from the private hell of the local garbage dump, be expected to fill in the conclusions of Jesus of Nazareth?

Look at the birds of the air: they neither sow nor reap nor gather into barns, and yet your heavenly Father feeds them. Are not you of more value than they? And which of you by being anxious can add one cubit to the span of his life? And why are you anxious about clothing? Consider the lilies of the field, how they grow; they neither toil nor spin; yet I tell you, even Solomon in all his glory was not arrayed like one of these. But if God so clothes the grass of the field, which today is alive and tomorrow is thrown into the oven, will he not much more clothe you, O men of little faith?

—Matt. 6:26-30

Presumably the disciples of Jesus were at the moment clothed and fed. Their problem was the shadow of insecure tomorrows bringing anxiety into the present. It is one problem to convince a chronic worrier that tomorrow's threats will never materialize; it is quite another to convince today's victim that he is not a victim.

In the early conversations, Job seems to see himself a baffling exception to the general rule. Later, he believes that he is a dramatic example of a general miscarriage of justice. Is the force of the presence of God, reminding him of what he already knew during the dialogue, sufficient to cause Job to accept his present lot as good, contrary to all experience?

It would then be possible for Job to have an answer without being told. The sufficiency of God, accepted

101

through faith rather than experience, would be discovered and appropriated, rather than as instinctively received, without alternative, by animals.

### MAN'S HONOR IN HISTORY

Should Job thus find himself in a sense a creature of God, but a creature whose own will and intelligence were necessary to complete the span of providential care, he would discover in man a dignity apart from all other life. Confronting God apart from the force of natural process, he assumes that the ends of the processes of nature will in some strange way be fulfilled in him. God will not deal with him by pulling switches or pressing buttons, pressing him into a mold. God will deal with him in response to the outreaching of his mind and the unpredictable darting of his imagination.

Man is not dealt with as a creature in God's speech. Both Job and his friends look to a creature category as ideal, supposing the purring of comfortable souls under the tender strokes of a divine hand to be ultimate beatitude. Job is amazed that anyone could treat the work of his own hands as God has treated him.

> Thy hands fashioned and made me;
> and now thou dost turn about and destroy me.
> Remember that thou hast made me of clay;
> and wilt thou turn me to dust again?
> —10:8-9

However, were Job simply the creature of God, there would be no voice from the storm. Wild creatures live, thrive, generate, suffer, and die. So far as anyone can tell, their protests are to the world around them, not to the emptiness above. What they can see, they can know. Not granted the boon of cosmic ignorance, of the encircling void of the not known, they cannot appeal to the lurking Possibility that has always been the curse and the hope of man.

That God comes and speaks to Job is in itself a guarantee to Job that he is a "somebody." He is neither comfortable nor fulfilled. His experience violates his idea of what life ought to be. But he does exist before God; there is somehow under the surface mockery of God's speech the emergence of a new, unsuspected, indefinable alternative. Job is being invited to seize this new alternative without knowing how it will turn out.

The clearest indication that God considers Job a responsible person rather than a defective creature whose machinery needs readjusting is found in a brief interjection between the two main sections of speech from the storm. When God closes his first series of questions challenging Job's knowledge, he receives the reply,

> Behold, I am of small account;
>     what shall I answer thee?
> I lay my hand on my mouth.
> I have spoken once, and I will not answer;
>     twice, but I will proceed no further.
> —40:4-5

Dissatisfied with this noncommittal answer, God opens a second interview in which he challenges Job to justify his pretensions.

> Deck yourself with majesty and dignity;
>     clothe yourself with glory and splendor.
> Pour forth the overflowing of your anger,
>     and look on every one that is proud,
>         and abase him.
> Look on every one that is proud,
>     and bring him low;
>     and tread down the wicked
>         where they stand.

> Hide them all in the dust together;
> bind their faces in the world below.
> Then will I also acknowledge to you,
> that your own right hand can give you victory.
> —40:10-14

The glory here ironically ascribed to Job is the glory proper to God. Job has attributed to God alone the capacity to humble all human greatness (12:13-25). At the same time, he has attributed all wisdom and might to God (12:13). As has been pointed out, however, God is here speaking to the whole human race, of which Job is representative; he is really speaking past Job to the audience who by now have identified themselves with him. Man has been unable to fulfill his standards of justice in the freedom given him to form the structures of society. Who is he to accuse God of mismanagement of the universe? He is unable to take care of his own back yard; how can he challenge the God who deals so adequately with star and flower? God, having made man free, does not accept total responsibility for history. Let man demand the blueprints of providence when he is able to display to God any intelligent purpose in the dark complications of his own attempts to direct history.

Pride and self-sufficiency, rather than moral disorder, are the basic indictments which God places on society. It is man's false view of himself that is the real social disease. So far, this disease has raged beyond man's control. The Job whose integrity, in the sense of personal righteousness, has sustained him with a fierce inner energy through all his trials and whose final posture is to stand like a prince before God, has at the last fallen, like a mighty Moses before the rock of temptation, into sin. His sin has not been the rejection of God prophesied by Satan; it has rather been that he dictates terms to God.

104

## MAN'S HONOR BEFORE GOD

When man insists upon coming to terms with God simply on the basis of mutually discharged obligations leading to mutually desirable ends, he destroys the creative force of history. Sophocles profoundly observes that "sometimes justice itself is fraught with harm" (*Electra*, p. 164). Job has asked God to be just; what in his agony he has been receiving has indeed not been justice. But human experience may not so much fall short of justice as go beyond it. Under the impulse of terrible new forces, Job has already been compelled to explore realms otherwise undreamed of. He has been a pilgrim in a new land of self-realization, of terrible existential truth, a land neither deserved nor undeserved. Nor was it merely accidental, flatly separated from what had gone before. After all, the prologue makes clear that it is the very goodness of Job that makes him a candidate for his new experience. The response to his pain, the very depth of his outrage has been conditioned by his former state. Only one who has risen high can plunge to profound depths. Only one who has known the thrill of belonging can savor the full bitterness of alienation.

When God refuses to accept the closed system of alternatives presented to him in Job's challenge, he implicitly gives Job the opportunity to accept a new role. Job can surrender without negotiation. He can accept God's way even if this means that the ashes of Uz remain his ultimate destiny. He can accept the right because it is right, even knowing the horror that might continue to attend it.

The new alternative emerging for Job is created by his trials. The issue on which the test began was whether man was good because he found it to his profit or because of his unselfish devotion to the will of God. In the process of the dialogue, one luminous, positive certainty emerges from all his searchings: the certainty, not simply of his integrity, but of the justifying force of integrity in itself. As has been pointed out, a glance at the list of moral ideals in chapter 31 makes clear that there is a categorical right which transcends the immediate effects of human action and is grounded in God.

> If I have rejected the cause of my
> manservant or my maidservant,
> when they brought a complaint against me;
> what then shall I do when God rises up?
> When he makes inquiry, what shall I answer him?
> Did not he who made me in the womb make him?
> And did not one fashion us in the womb?
> —31:13-15

Job is good to his slave not simply because he would be a better slave but because God made them both the same way; human equality is a fact only before an inscrutable Creator God who has *his* purposes in the incubation of each identity. Job also points out that he cared for the help-less because otherwise he "would not have faced his [God's] majesty" (31:23b).

The pride which makes Job liable to the judgment of God and the pride which holds Job's world together are two sides of the same coin. With the withdrawal of the God of pious tradition, Job has in fact enthroned a new God to replace him: the God of that which is right in itself. He is willing to submit his case, side by side with the God who has mistreated him, to this ephemeral, improbable new majesty.

Job clings to God as he ought to be, but not to God. He wants God to be and to do the right as Job himself under-stands it. When the God of his traditional definition of justice—a rigid cause-and-effect system binding the acts of men to a preconceived, mechanical fulfillment—aban-dons him, Job turns to the powerless, helpless "Right in

Itself." He gives his allegiance to the umpire for whom there are no credentials, to the advocate who remains silent through the trial, to the brother-redeemer whose sword remains in its sheath. Job gives his heart to a God who fails to manifest in history and experience inescapable credentials of divinity or majesty.

### THE HONOR BEYOND MAN

In his quest, Job does not lose God; he loses the image of the God who, sufficient for easy days, is put to the test while Job is tested. Both, in a sense, have been found wanting; a new Job is now able to communicate with a new God.

The rebel of Uz discovers God without knowing it. Unwilling to violate the plain significance of human history and his own experience to protect the faceless image of the old justice, in the honesty of his despair he plunges to new foundations. Satan's question is answered. He did not ask whether Job would remain theologically correct; he asked whether he would serve God for naught. The trial which follows, whatever Satan supposes it might be, is not simply the assaying of gold nuggets already present; it becomes the crucible in which the gold is refined. The trials are Job's opportunity—his first opportunity—to know God somehow in himself, apart from crown, scepter, and cherubim. Consequently the test becomes a dynamic thing, creative and productive.

It is possible theoretically to say that man can never reject God when he appears as objective, proven majesty. One might as well, standing righteously in the middle of the tracks, refuse to accept the approach of an off-schedule freight train. Just so one can hardly accept a God of phenomenal majesty, associated with earthquakes, volcanoes, or the seasons. Similarly, a God embodied in demonstrable logical conclusions, or in a self-contained dialectical system containing answers to all human problems, cannot be escaped. A sophisticated mind can be overwhelmed by logical force just as a simpler mind bows to the force of the phenomenal.

Man is free to accept God only without overt coercion. Very God may not appear therefore as the mightiest force in experience. To serve him may not seem to be sensible. The acceptance of God may appear the least attractive, the least plausible, of all presented alternatives. But the unaccountable attraction of the right-in-itself, which may appear quite absurd on the surface of life, continues to beckon; and though by all canons of sound sense and self-interest honor is powerless, it may in its weakness conquer us.

Job's difficulty is that the identity of his new God is based in himself. His own sense of cosmic housekeeping therefore becomes normative as to the order of things. His conscience is the pillar and ground of the universe. Job needs to be freed from the half-truth of his new idolatry, so that he may sense the God who is beyond himself— the right that transcends definition. Then he may live by the faith to which mystery is a precondition and human need a prophecy. Thus God's speech draws Job away not so much from his ideas as from the self-centeredness which imprisons them.

> Will you even put me in the wrong?
> Will you condemn me that you
> may be justified?
>
> —40:8

God turns Job's eyes to a world outside himself—a world which goes on, as it were, oblivious of the importance of man, resistant to his inquiries, and unsusceptible to his management. In the orderliness of natural phenomena there is something forever apart from man, something indomitable and intractable.

In the accounts of Behemoth (40:15-24) and Leviathan (41:1-34) God shows Job supreme examples of creatures that may not be tamed. The ancient myth that the world was formed from the corpse of the defeated dragon may have left the lingering impression, strengthened by natural disasters, that the earth is itself a living, intractable thing. Man rides it in triumph for a bit and then, in spite of all his efforts, is flung carelessly to one side. The placid surface of this planet conceals an unmanageable bronco.

While it is true today that any hippopotamus or crocodile, as well as any monster of the sea, is easy prey to man's new weapons, the threat they posed has not vanished. As described, they seem to be a strange combination of known animals and mythological beasts. At least no animal known to naturalists, including Tyrannosaurus, was ever able to kindle coals with his breath (41:21). Actually, the following lines describe the steam locomotive better than the crocodile.

> His sneezings flash forth light,
>   and his eyes are like the eyelids
>     of the dawn.
> Out of his mouth go flaming torches;
>   sparks of fire leap forth.
> Out of his nostrils comes forth smoke,
>   as from a boiling pot and burning
>     rushes.
>
> —41:17-20

Seeing the similarity of Leviathan to a modern machine, one is reminded of the irony that man, who has disposed well enough of whale and crocodile, is now astride more implacable monsters of his own devisings. Dynamite, electricity and atom: perhaps only God can put the bit in *these*.

Monsters symbolized the pathos of man's inadequacy amidst his surroundings. They continue to be spawned by new breakthroughs in technology and invention, giants infesting today's Canaan. Since the first weed created when man violated earth with a hoe and fertilized it with sweat (cf. Gen. 3:17-19), man has continually been confronted with the untameable. Leviathan, the eternal dragon, constantly changes shape and aspect; but his frightening, plunging, apparently irresponsible power remains forever the same. He may still be sensed in flood and earthquake, wind and fire, as ancient rabbis once heard him groan weirdly in Mediterranean fogs. His voice may be heard in the growl of a mob or the battle shout of a barbarian army, overrunning some new Rome.

Behemoth and Leviathan are not pleasant creatures; one immediately senses the incongruity of parading these toothy, cavorting giants before the eyes of a sick man. The parade is no more incongruous, however, than the spectacle of today's starving and baffled world, cowering under the threat of nuclear war, and sick of new lesions created by the cures of the old.

Man is liable to get the impression that there is something about this world that doesn't like him and will not submit to him. God, it must be remembered, has not addressed him as a creature. God may slap the rump of Leviathan and make a plaything of Behemoth, but he *talks* to man. He holds him responsible. Job must be something of an alien in the universe to be a companion of God. To sink back into natural law and resume his creaturely role, living even by the sublimely rationalized instinct of justice, is really to lose freedom, to lose self, to lose God.

Man is not to rest his hopes upon negotiating a system in which God and he act together in justice because, for man, there can be no justice. Human experience is so

110

complex, so much the result of interacting forces beyond
the control of man, that no judge can assign to offenders
what they precisely deserve for their crime. Similarly,
just rewards for virtue cannot be computed. True, natural
consequences, often predictable, will follow any action.
Few will claim, however, that such consequences in themselves meet the demands of justice.

"A tooth for a tooth" is only superficially just. One tooth
was broken out on impulse, the other in deliberation. One
victim had no premonition (any more, perhaps, than his
assailant) that a tooth would be lost; the luckless assailant
had long moments of unhappy anticipation before the
books were balanced. These experiences do not balance.
Legal systems properly struggle to correct the deficiences of
natural law in order to create a workable discipline within
society, but justice is a myth. When a man is punished,
very frequently he so adjusts his moral universe that the
penalty is experienced as persecution. The executioner
punishes, receiving the benefit of such satisfactions as
correcting the oversights of providence may give him. The
victim, however, is not *punished*; he is martyred.

Many will suppose that without retribution there can
be no moral law. Actions would not have consequences
relating to their rightness or wrongness, nor would God
by intervention fashion a general moral order.

Actions, however, still have consequences. These consequences simply cannot be described satisfactorily as rewards or punishments. Experiences consequent to dishonorable actions may really appear to be desirable. Observers
may be unable to discover any evidence of effective judgment in the aftermath of sin. This does not mean that
there is no judgment, nor that moral effects are unrelated to
causes. It simply means that the consequences of man's
deeds, whether we understand them simply as "cause
and effect" or as assigned directly by God, are frequently

111

irreconcilable with any discernible system of punishments and rewards. In the effects of many evil actions there may be discerned, in the grace of God, unexpected traces of honor still bravely shining. Emerging in the wake of man's best moments can similarly be found unexpected signals of peril.

It is true that Job's acceptance of the will of God comes while he is under severe indictment for his mistaken judgments about God. No threats are made, however. He repents because he has seen God; his views are inconsistent with the God he now knows, so he abandons them. Job's reckless assertions, culminating as they do in the appearance of God, are both frightful and wonderful. God's coming is neither reward nor punishment, but a consequence of man's creative outcries.

That God comes to Job indicates that something was right about what Job did. His stated conclusions are faulty largely because of self-centeredness and the inadequacy of inherited views to explain the terrible new world into which he had been flung. But his struggle toward God puts him in a new dimension of experience where he becomes able for the first time to come to terms with the inexcusable madness of his world without the loss of honor.

# VI

# Elihu: Exegete Extraordinary of Storms and Sermons

Should the poetry of Job consist simply of the conversations of Job and his three friends, followed by God's speech, the impact of the work would depend almost entirely upon the reader's ability to look past the text. The indirection of the Voice from the Whirlwind demands, for proper interpretation, that one reach beyond the periphery of the storm to the still small voice at the heart of tumult.

> Lo, these are but the outskirts of his ways;
> and how small a whisper do we
> hear of him!
> But the thunder of his power
> who can understand?
> —26:14

Since the Book of Job is artistically conceived and constructed, the reader must lend the author his imagination; he must project himself into the arena he is watching.

One artistic dimension used by the poet of Job is that of debate. God's speech emphasizes the futility of debate as a means of solving the riddles of the justice of God in the paradoxes of history. God speaks not so much argumentatively as peremptorily. He does not intend to enter the debate so much as to show its irrelevance.

Should a reader therefore suppose that debate and argument must provide logical answers to the problem of unmerited suffering, he would be frustrated with God's speech. God indeed wins, and Job recants. But it appears that the outcome is determined by the sheer force of divine majesty. God had recourse, when actually worsted in the debate, to his fists. Job cries "Uncle!" "At last from sheer fatigue he dropped his sword and fell fainting; for he a mortal frail, dared to wage war upon a god." (Euripides *The Bacchantes*, p. 345.) So understood, the Book of Job intensifies rather than solves its problem. God triumphs in dishonor. He has intended to show that man would serve him without reward; in point of fact he has coerced a confession from the helpless victim of his own unjustifiable assaults.

The employment of Satan in the prologue as a buffer figure between God and human catastrophe is not taken seriously in the poetry. Job knows nothing of the transaction, nor does a chagrined Satan appear in the epilogue to show Job who the adversary really was. God remains responsible for the calamities of the poetry, but in his speech he says nothing to justify their occurrence.

#### THE GOD WHO REVEALS

The Elihu speeches appear to be the attempt of an earnest pedagogue to rescue God from his own power. The three friends, as the brief prologue to Elihu's speeches points out, had failed to defend God adequately (32:3). Job had "justified himself rather than God" (32:2). The friends' silence confesses that Job's arguments are, humanly speaking, unanswerable; only God can confute him.

Beware lest you say, "We have
found wisdom;
God may vanquish him, not man."
—32:13

Elihu insists that the weakness of Job's position may be exposed by proper arguments.

The new speaker bursts on the scene with irrepressible, bombastic confidence. He has suffered exquisitely in listening to a bungled debate.

Behold, my heart is like wine that has no vent;
Like new wineskins, it is ready to burst.
—32:19

Protocol had demanded that he remain silent. Now that Job and the friends cease, Elihu impatiently presents his case.

It is hard to tell whether or not the reader is intended to be amused by the pretentious throat-clearings of this youth. Through all of chapter 32 and part, if not all, of chapter 33 he announces that he is about to say something. I think, however, that the author writes in what is to him a fundamentally serious vein, and any humor is largely unintentional (though nonetheless real to the reader for all that!)

One can easily imagine a modern youth, whose mind is clear because it is uncluttered with information, breezily setting his elders to rights on world affairs, religion, and science. It would indeed be inexcusable for him to emerge with a better solution than those of reverend and elaborately confused doctors.

The new, self-confident, young speaker intends to draw the truth of God out of the realm of the intuitional, where one grasps at the unspoken or hinted purposes of God, and justify them by argument. While the speeches of Elihu are hard to put in a logical progression, within their fragments they show close, coherent argument quite superior to that of the friends. God is acting reasonably, and the man who thinks correctly can understand his purposes.

Elihu considers himself peculiarly able to enlighten Job. He is not cumbered with the misconceptions of the past.

> It is not the old that are wise,
> nor the aged that understand
> what is right.
>
> —32:9

He is antitraditionalist. Today's truth is not to be found in the epigrams of an idealized past.

Elihu's authority rests upon something more immediate. He has been granted the inward perceptions of the breath of God, or the Spirit. His youth will testify for him, for he will be wiser than aged scholars; his precocity is the gift of God.

> But it is the spirit in a man,
> the breath of the Almighty,
> that makes him understand.
>
> . . . . . . . . .
>
> For I am full of words,
> the spirit within me constrains
> me.
>
> —32:8, 18

He speaks with telling conviction, for his ideas are first-hand. Sincerity is the fruit of communication with very God.

> My words declare the uprightness of my heart,
> and what my lips know they speak sincerely.
> The Spirit of God has made me,
> and the breath of the Almighty gives me life.
>
> —33:3-4

When Elihu claims to explain the mysteries of God to Job through inspiration or intuition, the charge might be made that God is using a man as a mouthpiece by which to smuggle contraband information to Job. Thus he will be able to endure the test triumphantly while Satan remains baffled by his unaccountable fortitude. A fence would again be erected around the beloved of God, whose righteousness would continue to be the result of informed self-interest.

Elihu does not, however, bring new data to Job. He interprets events that are common to the experience of men. Dreams, suffering, the rise and fall of mighty men, the impartial sickle of death, and the raging, healing storm are a part of general experience. As interpreter he draws forth lessons available to all who would investigate.

Elihu indeed claims that he has access to God inwardly, but it is an access common to all men! The "breath of the Almighty" gives understanding (32:8); this "breath" or "spirit" is his because God made him (33:4), not because of a special spiritual experience. Elihu speaks a wisdom anyone could have if he rightly searched for God.

In the development of his argument, it becomes apparent that Elihu really refers to the rational capacity of man. He does what the beast cannot do: he utilizes the deductive possibilities of reason itself to build a self-consistent understanding of God. Specific evidence, jeopardized by unreliable observation and interpretation, is no longer final. God's truth survives all the apparent contradictions of experience; it proclaims the ultimate, understandable sanity of the ways of God with man. Elihu can be antitraditionalist because he has access always to the sublime inward certainties of the rational mind.

For Elihu, the glory of man is to *know*; the fundamental purpose of God is to *reveal*. The ideal man is gnostic;

understanding the hidden meanings of God, he is enabled to govern his life thereby. To act arrogantly proceeds from ignorance of God, from a misconstruction of divine actions.

As has been seen, Job has asked for an umpire, one who in some sense would mediate the ways of God to him, and his ways to God (cf. 9:33). He needed someone who would have authority over both himself and God, so that justice might exist in divine-human relations (cf. 16:21). Elihu does not, of course, claim such authority, but he does claim close access to God (9:32), as well as sympathetic understanding of man.

> Behold, I am toward God as you are;
> I too was formed from a piece of clay.
> Behold, no fear of me need terrify you;
> my pressure will not be heavy
> upon you.
>
> —33:6-7

He does not intend to correct Job by threats or violence; he intends to persuade him by discourse.

It is further clear that Elihu is placed in a mediatorial position in the structure of the book. Job closes in an address to God; Elihu speaks; God responds to Job. Elihu begins by reference to the dialogue; he ends with the description of the storm. Whether or not he is supposed to be describing the approaching whirlwind (37:21-24) there is little question but that this aspect of his speech is related to the nature content of God's answer.

I think the extraordinary passage describing the saving function of the mediator (33:19-28) may in fact be a reference to Elihu himself. There is no question but that he thinks highly of his ability to interpret God. In all of chapter 33 he insists that God does communicate with man; it is his own business to be the agent of such communication.

First, God communicates through dreams, though man may not understand them.

> For God speaks in one way,
>     and in two, though man does not
>         perceive it.
> In a dream, in a vision of the night,
>     when deep sleep falls upon men,
>     while they slumber on their beds.
>                                         —33:14-15

Should the dream fail, God speaks to man through his suffering. This, too, he may misunderstand. If, however, he has an "angel" or mediator, he may be led so to understand what is happening that his suffering becomes his ransom (cf. 36:18) and he is delivered from imminent death.

When Elihu finishes recounting to Job the present possibility of his rescue through the good offices of "an angel, a mediator, one of the thousand," (33:23b) he invites Job to listen to him.

> Give heed, O Job, listen to me;
>     be silent, and I will speak.
> If you have anything to say, answer me;
>     speak, for I desire to justify you.
> If not, listen to me;
>     be silent, and I will teach you
>         wisdom.
>                                         —33:31-33

He never mentions the method of rescue and restoration again.

It seems incredible that Job's one real hope of healing should be so clearly raised only to be abandoned. Could it not be that the remainder of Elihu's remarks simply "declare to man what is right for him" (33:23c) with the understanding that restoration and reconciliation will follow, should Job accept the truth? Chapters 34 through 37 are then properly devoted to justifying God's ways to Job, so that he might repent and be healed. To describe the *manner* in which Job would negotiate with God for release from suffering and restoration to honor in the community would not be Elihu's business.

The "mediator" speech of Elihu does suggest what might be termed a cultic (or sacramental) procedure. That he "comes into his presence with joy" (33:26b) resembles in vocabulary and intention a worshiper's approach to God in his temple; subsequent testimony (in psalm) before man (33:26-27) similarly suggests the presentation of a thank offering by a healed and forgiven penitent. But the whole intent of the poetry of Job is to deal with the ways of God with men outside the practices of formal religion. Whether Elihu is himself the mediator of this cultic salvation may be debated; but it is clear that he intends to bring Job the inner enlightenment without which no restoration could be available to him.

Elihu is indeed a mediator. But he is not consciously the "umpire" which Job said he needed. The umpire causes both God and man to submit to the demands of justice. For Elihu, as shall be seen, God is beyond law. He interprets God to Job, but does not need to interpret Job to God.

Elihu emphasizes that God *reveals* things to men. Man is intended to understand the strategy of heaven and consciously to relate himself to it. Such knowledge is not simply written down in books or embodied in wise saws. It is manifest in happenings in which God reaches toward man—such as dreams and suffering. It is explained by clear-minded, inspired interpreters able to outline the strategy of a rational, moral God.

For Elihu, the glory of man is his rationality, his capacity to grasp the sublime logic of all the doings of God. Admittedly, the sufferings of mankind pose a formidable threat to this rationalistic faith. Elihu is prepared not only to defend God's general strategy in human affairs but also to show that it is in man's suffering that God's purposes are most profound and effective.

### THE IMPARTIAL JUSTICE OF GOD

The foundation stone of all Elihu's dialectic, his self-sufficient chain of arguments dealing with Job's case, is the impartiality of God. The divine nature can be neither capricious nor arbitrary. God might appear thus to confused thinking, but to the clear mind all the works of God are absolutely just.

God governs the universe; the natural order subsists in him. He alone is responsible for the world, and for its continued substantiality.

> Who gave him charge over the earth
> and who laid on him the whole
> world?
> If he should take back his spirit
> to himself,
> and gather to himself his breath,
> all flesh would perish together,
> and man would return to dust.
> —34:13-15

Is it logical to suppose that one who thus governs his own property hates justice? He shows no respect for human pretensions and treats rich and poor impartially.

> Shall one who hates justice govern?
> Will you condemn him who is
> righteous and mighty,
> who says to a king, "worthless one,"
> and to nobles, "wicked man";

> who shows no partiality to princes,
>     nor regards the rich more than
>         the poor,
>     for they are all the work of his hands?
>         —34:17-19

Death is assigned to all; it delays for no dignitary.

> In a moment they die;
>     at midnight the people are
>         shaken and pass away,
>     and the mighty are taken away
>         by no human hand.
>         —34:20

That God governs what is, after all, *his* proper estate with majestic disregard for human pretention argues that he is absolutely just.

Elihu acclaims the impartiality of God on other grounds. God is higher above man than the clouds; he can be coerced neither by wickedness, which does not affect him (35:6) nor by righteousness, which does not profit him (35:7). Euripides too understands that very God must be beyond needs. He says: "For the deity, if he be really such, has no wants; these are miserable fictions of the poets." (*Heracles Mad*, p. 376.) Man's actions have consequences simply for himself.

> Your wickedness concerns a man
>     like yourself,
>     and your righteousness a son of man.
>         —35:8

Thus God does not act for what might be called *personal* reasons. He is not provoked to unwarrantedly destructive anger by human mischief, nor is he softened to extraordinary leniency by subservience. "For those answers we strive to extort from heaven . . . are goods that bring no blessing on our getting; but what they freely offer, thereby we profit." (Euripides *Ion*, p. 285.)

Actually, God's might is the guarantee of his justice, for it puts him beyond all the fear and selfishness which, in vulnerable man, leads to the corruption of justice. One who is a billionaire is not to be bribed by nickels. A Khrushchev cannot be intimidated by the threats of Tibetans. Chattering monkeys do not keep the elephant from seeking the foliage needed to satisfy his massive appetite. So God is beyond the threats and importunities of men. Detached from dependence upon citizens who subsist upon the creative surge of his breath, God alone can be the administrator of absolute justice.

> Behold, God is mighty, and does not despise any;
> he is mighty in strength of understanding.
> —36:5

In brief, might makes right.

Elihu therefore inverts the arguments Job advanced in chapter 9, where he asserted that the greatness of a God beyond sanction made justice for man categorically impossible. God, says Elihu, is sufficiently detached from the world of men to be impartial. Just retribution derives inevitably from his nature.

> For according to the work of a man he will requite him,
> and according to his ways he will make it befall him.
> —34:11

Elihu is therefore a retributionist even beyond the friends, who seemed to leave some room for God's unaccountable whims. His problem now is to explain to Job how the God who is in essence absolute justice could have treated him with such brutality. He does not follow the argument of the three friends that Job was a gross sinner and deserved his fate. On the contrary, he insists that God afflicts Job in order to speak to him.

## THE HEALING WOUNDS OF GOD

The following statement illustrates the basic difference between Elihu's approach and that of the friends.

> He delivers the afflicted by their affliction,
> and opens their ear by adversity.
> —36:15

The friends would surely say, "He delivers the afflicted *from* their affliction." God is prevailed upon to rescue those who approach him properly. But Elihu insists that there is a Process working *within* human experience which saves man: God need not approach from without. God is already working with Job; in fact, while Job has been complaining of his absence, God has called for him in the terrible urgency of pain.

Here Elihu brings forward a concept clearly implied in God's speech. God is in the order of things! To describe the government of the universe is to describe the providence of God for persons.

Elihu's description of the world of nature, and especially the function of storms, illustrates how catastrophe relates to providence. In God's speech from the whirlwind moralizings must come from the reader. Elihu insists on spelling out his own applications. Storms judge men, for lightning strikes some and warns others of him "who is jealous with anger against iniquity" (36:33*b*). At the same time, however, the rains give "food in abundance" (36:31*b*). The same clouds perform at one and the same time the multiform business of God.

124

> They turn round and round by his guidance,
> to accomplish all that he commands them
>   on the face of the habitable world.
> Whether for correction, or for his land,
>   or for love, he causes it to happen.
> —37:12-13

Just so the lightning of his anger opens up the rain clouds of his mercy. The hammer blows of divine wrath are part and parcel of showers of blessing.

The storm of affliction is visited upon wicked and righteous men alike. The wicked are not kept alive, but the afflicted receive their right (36:6). The righteous are frequently exalted with kings (36:7); but sometimes they themselves are afflicted:

> He does not withdraw his eyes from
>   the righteous,
> but with kings upon the throne
> he sets them for ever, and they are exalted.
> And if they are bound in fetters
>   and caught in the cords of affliction,
> then he declares to them their work
>   and their transgressions, that
>     they are behaving arrogantly.
> —36:7-9

Such righteous people fulfill formal canons of behavior but fall prey to the sin of pride. The favor of God is misconstrued as favoritism. Only by withdrawing his favor can God save his own from self-destructive arrogance. Those who think they can presume on God must be warned of spiritual peril.

Perceptive men sense the warning in their affliction and are restored.

> If they hearken and serve him,
> they complete their days in

125

> prosperity,
> and their years in pleasantness.
>
> —36:11

If they fail to heed the warning, affliction becomes punishment—a foretaste of ultimate terror.

> But if they do not hearken, they perish by the sword,
> and die without knowledge.
>
> —36:12

Whether he is blessed or cursed by his affliction is strictly up to the sufferer himself. What might have been his punishment may indeed function as a ransom; Elihu later observes, "Let not the greatness of the ransom turn you aside" (36:18*b*). Presumably the greater the suffering, the greater the blessing may be. The more poignant man's agony the more profoundly he may sense the meanings of God.

Some men make suffering an occasion for reviling God.

> The godless in heart cherish anger;
> they do not cry for help when he binds
> them.
>
> —36:13

They enthrone resentment and cut off from themselves the possibility of reconciliation with God. Outrage alone never saved anybody.

> But none says, "Where is God my Maker,
> who gives songs in the night,
> who teaches us more than the
> beasts of the earth,
> and makes us wiser than the birds
> of the air?"
>
> —35:10, 11

There is a human dignity in suffering; the victim inquires of God, the ultimate teacher, "What are you saying to me?" God is not dealing with man as he deals with the world of nature. Man is more complex; uniquely responsible, he searches as he responds.

Elihu insists that Job experiences affliction as do the wicked. He has stubbornly refused to learn what God is saying. Since man is equipped to know the will of God, Job's sin is that of willful ignorance. He is so insensitive that God's most pointed arrows fail to pierce the cloak of his self-sufficiency. Job has indeed cried out—but not in inquiry or faith. He has attempted, presumptuously, to negotiate with an impartial God!

> There they cry out, but he does not answer,
>    because of the pride of evil men.
> Surely God does not hear an empty cry,
>    nor does the Almighty regard it.
> How much less when you say that
>    you do not see him,
>    that the case is before him, and
>    you are waiting for him!
>             —35:12-14

Elihu, the interpreter of God, therefore sternly accuses Job of wrong thinking, thinking that makes him an ally of the hopelessly wicked.

> But you are full of the judgment
>    on the wicked;
>    judgment and justice seize you.
> Beware lest wrath entice you into scoffing;
>    and let not the greatness of the
>    ransom turn you aside.
>             —36:17-18

The moral energy of Job's cry will not save him (36:19). Determining what his sufferings will be, he has chosen unwisely.

> Take heed, do not turn to iniquity,
>   for this you have chosen rather
>     than affliction.
>
> —36:21

Whether the affliction becomes corrosive depends upon how one receives it. Those who read the purpose of God on pages of anguish are alerted to impending moral disaster.

The depth of human suffering testifies to the depth of ignorance through which God must reach to get man's ear. A freezing man may have to be cuffed from the deceptive numbness of approaching death into the agony of returning life. A man whose house is on fire is rarely gently awakened. Cauterization often reaches deep to bring healing. Elihu insists that the love of God strikes man down to bring him to the very edge of the Pit (33:22). Love is given impartially to man; whether it brings redemptive insight or damning bitterness is up to man himself.

For man to run afoul of trouble does not rob him of initiative. Pain does not negate responsibility. For the wise —that is, good—man, pain and sorrow present a new opportunity for the soul's inquiry toward the will of God. Job need not be a helpless organism whimpering under torture. He has the alternative of speaking past his struggle· "So you *are* real, then! What are you saying to me?"

#### JUSTICE BEYOND SHEOL

Elihu differs from the friends and Job in that he does not insist that death is the same terminus for all. While the wicked suffer in this life and the good are blessed, there is no observable balancing between moral cause and effect. The tribulation necessary to bring a man to his senses may violate justice. How can Elihu continue to assert divine retribution?

It appears to me that, for Elihu, the death that awaits the sinner resolves any question that might remain concerning the justice of his treatment in history. On the other hand, the righteous is granted a life beyond death which justifies the afflictions necessary to attain it.

Elihu points out to Job that God reveals himself to man in dreams; such terrifying experiences are intended to turn man away from perilous paths, so that he might avoid death (33:13-17).

> He keeps back his soul from the pit,
> his life from perishing by the sword.
> —33:18

In his description of redemption in chapter 33, Elihu shows how the sufferer is brought to the very edge of the Pit.

> His soul draws near the Pit,
> and his life to those who
> bring death.
> —33:22

Thus enlightened, he hears the announcement, "Deliver him from going down into the Pit" (33:24b). He becomes young again (33:25) and goes into the presence of God (33:26). He testifies of his salvation, concluding,

> He has redeemed my soul from going down into the Pit,
> and my life shall see the light.
> —33:28

Elihu comments further,

> Behold, God does all these things,
> twice, three times, with a man,
> to bring back his soul from the Pit,
> that he may see the light of life.
> —33:29-30

Just as the *Pit* is the destination to be avoided, so is *life* the objective to be gained. It is noteworthy that in 32:28-30 life and light are both placed in opposition to the Pit, which is of course associated with darkness. A question inevitably arises: Is the life-or-death contrast in Elihu's teaching simply that of traditional Hebrew thinking? If death is a common fate, if Sheol knows no distinctions, how are the righteous ultimately distinguished from the wicked? Do the repentant simply get a new lease on life, so that, like King Hezekiah, they get a few more years of happiness?

It is hard to see God going to great pains to save man from a Pit to which he is in any event ultimately destined. The logic of Elihu seems therefore to demand differentiation *after* death. The "life" to which man is delivered would properly be everlasting, or uninterrupted. Thus the justice of God would ultimately be served beyond earthly time; apparent inequities would be rectified in the afterlife.

It should not be supposed that this "light of life" begins at death. It really begins when the afflicted man hears the voice of God in his suffering and turns back to an acceptance of God, rather than human status, as the ground of his being. Life after death becomes an extension of the imperishable status of renewed persons. Golden streets and gates of pearl are secondary to the new identity of which they are symbol. Surely he whose deadly sin was satisfaction in the temporal trappings of honor cannot save himself from *this* sin by any God-bribing disciplines of piety stemming from a desire to increase his holdings.

Only those for whom the delights of paradise are dispensable can enjoy Paradise.

Admittedly, there is little on the face of things in Elihu's pronouncements to suggest that he teaches retribution after this life. Man is, indeed, something more than the beasts of the earth (35:11). He is not to long for the night (36:20). But there are no descriptions of life after death, not even so much as Job's Sheol description. Nor does Elihu use the doctrine of judgment or vindication after death as a lever to move Job to his way of thinking.

There are, however, frequent references to escape from the Pit in the passage in which Elihu presents the possibility of salvation to Job (33:23 ff.). Once this possibility is put forward, Elihu concentrates his attention upon the justification of God's actions in this present world; therefore, references to life after death are unnecessary. God is right in his actions according to the unimpeachable order of things; Job is impelled to search into the truth of divine impartiality by the knowledge, given at the first, that life and death hang in the balance.

Oblique references to life after death seem to appear in the terminology of Elihu, however. For one thing, he never uses the term "Sheol" as the place of the dead. He rather uses the term "Pit." While it is true that the two terms are occasionally used in a parallel sense in the Old Testament, it appears that the Pit often has a connotation of disgrace, representing the end of a morally unworthy person. One may think of the Pit as a hole reserved for the wicked in the general cave of Sheol. Those who remain out remain relatively comfortable. Thus the new concept of differentiation in the state of the dead may have arisen.

Moreover, the life promised to Job by Elihu is not simple survival. When he reports the testimony of the redeemed sinner, he closes the account with the line, "And my life

131

shall see the light" (33:28*b*). In 30:30*b*, Elihu says the redeemed "may see the light of life," or possibly, "be lighted with the light of life."

The context of these passages is especially meaningful. The presence of God becomes the essence of life. A psalmist has written,

> For with thee is the fountain of life;
> in thy light do we see light.
> —Ps. 36:9

Elihu therefore promises new life for the redeemed; the word "light" emphasizes that the righteous are delivered not only *from* death, but *to* the joy saints know in the presence of God. This is in strong contrast to the dark fate of those who go down to the Pit.

Once it is granted that the "light of life" is in contrast to the darkness of the Pit, it is natural to wonder whether "light" is intended by Elihu to extend beyond the grave. In the "little apocalypse" of Isaiah we read,

> Thy dead shall live, their bodies shall rise.
> O dwellers in the dust, awake
> and sing for joy!
> For thy dew is a dew of light,
> and on the land of the shades
> thou wilt let it fall.
> —Isa. 26:19

The dew which resurrects the dead is called "a dew of light!" In the resurrection description in the Book of Daniel the angel says, "And those who are wise shall shine like the brightness of the firmament." (12:3.) The forty-ninth psalm, which clearly originates from the same point of view as that of Elihu, speaks of the ransom of helpless man from the power of death.

But God will ransom my soul from the power of Sheol,
   for he will receive me.
            —Ps. 49:15

The psalmist describes the unredeemed as those who "will never more see the light" (Ps. 49:19*b*). Euripides, too, began to sense the thrust of the demands of justice past the portals of death. "Yea, for there is recompense for these things as well amongst the dead as amongst all those who breathe the breath of life." (Euripides *Helen,* p. 307.)

In the light of general usage and local context, it seems clear that Elihu uses the expressions "light of life" or "light of the living" to describe the illumined existence of the redeemed in the presence of God. It is the antithesis of the darkness of death. There is no indication that any who experience this kind of life ever go to the Pit.

The glorified life includes present existence in history. So vigorous a hope does not readily submit to Sheol or the Pit. The Elihu speeches seem to show the Jewish mind at a point of transition from the flat, nondifferentiated "Sheol" view traditionally held to the clear heaven-hell contrast of later periods.

It is the moral radiance of the saved man before God that Elihu considers to be his proper honor. The resurrection—if that is what he implies—is secondary to the reception of divine grace and regenerative power. If one who walks with God simply cannot be conceived falling into the Pit, the great attainment remains reconciliation with God, with the capacity for radiant praise that marks the redeemed man.

To summarize, Elihu is really more concerned with a defense of the honor of God than with that of man. He is perceptive enough to see that God is not to be justified by invincible force. He attempts dialectically to show that God's force is, in essence, moral and just. His divinity and his position as creator and sustainer of all put him beyond the reach of any kind of coercion. He deals justly with men in that he is impartial; all receive the same treatment. That he dispenses suffering to all men is evidence of his mercy, for suffering opens up the possibility of new knowledge to man—knowledge by which he may avert unsuspected catastrophe and walk intelligently with God in the "light of life."

Man retains within himself the capacity to determine whether God shall be judge or savior. If he can discover the revelatory force of suffering, he can move into a new rapport with God. If in his stubbornness he insists upon resentment and rebellion, his pain becomes a foretaste of doom. What might have been a ransom becomes an execution.

Elihu did not consider himself to be an umpire in that he did not subject God to any standard of justice beyond himself. Yet the absolute detachment of God, his freedom from need, his serene noninvolvement, are in themselves reasonable new restrictions visited upon him by his acute defender. Where is *divine* initiative? Can he love anybody? Is his identity the awful blankness of the absolute Neuter?

Elihu believes that God bestows love upon man—as man makes himself a candidate for it. Just so he bestows anger on the proper candidates. But no one holding Elihu's views will suppose that God has seized him from his own worst self in spite of his efforts. Nor can one have a chance to accept an attack for which there is no explanation.

The fundamental sin of man is pride. The proud are characteristically unaware of mortal danger. God therefore brings man down to the Pit to show him the shallowness of his pretensions and the ineffectiveness of his independence. The pride that once was almost unnoticeable may harden into arrogance and overt rebellion. The sufferer insists that *God* is in the wrong. The interpreter rehabilitates the rebel by showing that individual suffering in no case compromises the impartiality of God. The rebel discovers opportunity rather than outrage in his anguish.

For Elihu, the proper honor of man is his existence in the presence of God as a healed and redeemed person. His honor is not the result of divine whim for without a voluntary, enlightened response he could never have attained it. The test offered by Satan is not compromised, for God has not departed from the general, impartial providence by which all temporal affairs are governed to save Job. Actually, the punishments suggested by Satan become the instruments of new revelation; God does not need to modify catastrophes for them to communicate to the sufferer.

Man cannot attain his status before God except as a knowing creature. Animals know God as sustainer, but man knows him as a teacher. The illumination of the mind precedes the cleansing of the spirit. The primal sin is ignorance; immorality derives from man's resistance to knowledge.

> "Job speaks without knowledge,
>   his words are without insight."
> Would that Job were tried to the end,
>   because he answers like wicked men.
> —34:35-36

What Job knows of God is available to all men, written large in the canon of experience. Interpreters speak indeed as God moves them, but the Spirit, the *charisma*, within them stirs in every human nostril. Those whose minds are not clouded by inherited bias or twisted by unjustifiable resentments can read the intention of God and confidently declare it to their fellows.

Human dignity, according to Elihu, is fully realized when a man finds it possible to dwell in the presence of a distant God who now, through a new perception, can be discovered in unlikely quarters. The God whose detachment from the human scene was the guarantee of his impregnable honesty suddenly appears immanent in immediate experiences. Enlightened humility permits man to find out that God is love, after all. Life's most terrible experiences pierce the gray sky with lightning and at the same time tilt waterskins over thirsty earth. God's impartial love is true to absolute justice. The honor of man would demand of such a love that it be available to others, or it could not properly reach him.

Satan had insisted that God had built a fence about Job. This was never denied. What Satan could not have known, in light of Elihu's view, was that his own attacks upon Job did not tear the fence down but, rather, completed it. Job's fence, compounded of bane and blessing, is now strung of such common stuff as no longer to be limited to the estates of comfortable saints. Far-flung as ubiquitous justice, the parapets of the love of God encircle the world.

# VII

# Epilogue: Rediscovery of Honor

When Satan had asked, "Does Job fear God for naught?" he received a first answer in the patient Job's response, "The Lord gave, and the Lord has taken away; blessed be the name of the Lord." (Job 1:9, 21.) Is the final pronouncement of the Job of the dialogue the same thing?

The resignation of the patient Job was rationalized. God gives and therefore has a right to take away (1:21). We receive good at the hand of the Lord, and we also receive evil (2:10). God is just in that all men receive the bitter and the sweet; what God has bestowed for no reason he may repossess for no reason. I return to the earth naked as I came; I start as nothing and end as nothing. The Job of the prologue finds the ultimate honor of man in his acceptance of his status as dust.

The rationalization which made it possible for Job to accept disaster hardly supports the honor of God. If he gives only to take away, if he clothes only to unclothe, if he gives good only to counterbalance giving evil, what then is his nature? Man is relegated to the status of a noble, articulate beast, while God remains irreproachable because there is no purpose from which he may fall short. The Job of the prose knows what God is doing, but the purpose of God for man does not rise beyond that for the

137

grass which "today is alive and tomorrow is thrown into the oven" (Matt. 6:30).

The prose vindicates God in the sense that the benediction, "Blessed be the name of the Lord!" suitable for grace at table and evening devotions during the good years, is unchanged at the end of his sufferings. The honor of man is that he persists and endures, unchanged by his experience.

When Job recants at the end of the poetry, he proclaims a purpose of God which, though he cannot justify, he accepts. He has attempted to understand that which was beyond understanding. "No purpose of thine can be thwarted. . . . I have uttered what I did not understand." (Cf. 42:2-3.) Because of his experience, something has happened; for the Job who had heard of God now sees him, and is enabled by the ultimate vision to respond in an acceptance expressive not of the piety existing when the test began, but of a capacity produced by the test itself!

God is now vindicated in that he has appropriated the test as a means by which the worth of man may be not simply assessed but created. He uses suffering, which seems to be least expressive of the worth of man, as a mediation of his ultimate worth. Job is permitted to explore the alternatives to resignation. His peace is not an extension of sublime, uninterrupted calm; it is the aftermath of an inner storm of which the revelatory whirlwind serves as a representation.

The thunder of the tornado was a voice because it was addressed to Job. His ears were attuned, as Elihu had prophesied, to meanings he could not have caught had he not been led to the gates of hell. Past the veil of mighty words Job caught the vision of God himself. The sounds which struck his ear mingled with the thunder of his pulse before he saw past sound and recognized the Friend who had eluded him.

That Job is able to accept a God whom he cannot understand argues that he has experienced faith. When he says he *sees* God, I think he means that beyond the rumors of philosophy and doctrine he has experienced a new divine reality. The mystery of the God he now accepts is a precondition of faith in him. Since Job accepts a God whose will is unpredictable, he cannot be accused of serving God calculatingly. Up to this point it appeared that to do God's will was to become liable to incalculable woe. Job's faith in God is not a mental projection of known consequences, on the basis of which man may sensibly act. It is a faith in God in himself; the only certain thing that may be said about God's purposes is that they are *his* purposes.

It may be argued that the final lines of Job's response, in which he says he despises himself, represent in the destruction of his worth the final loss of honor. Had Job simply been thundered into submission this would be the case; but as I have said, the translation of this passage is too uncertain to depend upon. It may have read, "Though I am melting away, I am comforted in regard to dust and ashes." (Cf. 42:6.) In this case the impact on the reader would be considerably changed. Job would now be asserting his worth.

Job's honor, in any case, does not rest upon his estimate of himself. It is not necessary, or perhaps even advantageous, that he say "my honor." He does not congratulate himself that he is worth a lot. Job's capacity, knowing God through experience, to find worth in God himself is the source of his honor. When a man says, "This is God's will," he does the right without conscious egoism and begins at the very center of his existence to take on the character of his Master. The right that is in God masters man in faith, not in the coercion of rewards and punishments, nor in the inescapable certainties of dialectical logic. Man comes to God in freedom. Therefore, even when he accepts God as the ultimate meaning and worth of his life, man is still a self. More properly, to the extent that he accepts God does he *become* a self.

The person who thinks only of himself is, to the extent that he is not distracted from his preoccupations, an identityless person. Only those outside themselves, only those capable of being charmed entirely away from self-consciousness can be real persons. The honor of Job is *his* only because he, understanding that he is related to something beyond himself, cannot claim it as his own. Since Job considers integrity of greater value than self, it can overcome all selfish considerations.

Faith becomes the means by which man's honor may be inward and at the same time related to a value greater than self. It is inward because faith is personal, not mechanical; it is more nearly a commitment than an acknowledgment. At the same time it draws man beyond himself because it asserts an Object upon which man is fundamentally dependent.

The prose epilogue which finishes the book at first appears to be an antithesis to the assertion of the poetry that reward is not necessary to righteousness. Job receives double indemnity for all lost possessions, and again has seven sons and three daughters. His old companions reappear—with gifts of money. Some would insist that the poet could not therefore have had the epilogue in mind when he wrote the play; he intended Job to expire, having been faithful at the last.

The epilogue does not, however, violate the rest of the book, for at least three reasons. First, God clearly insists in the prologue that Satan not take Job's life (2:6). Job must have at least an interim of health before he dies. Second, so far as Job is concerned, he has no intimation that he is going to be healed when he makes his recantation. Since Job did not repent in order to gain anything, he does not violate the test. Third, if God, in order to assert the fallacies of the doctrine of moral retribution, has to execute Job, he must submit to the grip of another closed system just as restrictive as before. God will have to be nonretributive! All good will have to produce disaster and all evil, happiness.

Having established that he is free to do as he chooses, God indeed can afflict Job. But he can also bless him without rewarding him. Vindication has been, from the standpoint of the poetry, Job's main concern. This accomplished, Job's honor is such that it is neither forwarded nor compromised by the accumulation of goods and the experience of happiness.

The epilogue is the dropping of the curtain upon the drama of Job. It is a half-step back from the cadenced artificiality of the dialogue to the everyday world, where the spectator begins to look for his gloves and car keys. Job and his friends slip back into stereotyped, unreal figures, creatures of a world of imagination remote from life as it is lived. Critics and theologians argue, students write themes, grammarians and linguists solemnly survey the remains of the play.

The curtain has fallen and the play is over—so far as anything can be completed which is interpretative of one's own heart's blood.

## VIII

# Intimations from the Ashes of Uz

There is no solution, in the sense of words and ideas, to the problem of Job. It could be said that Elihu solves the problems defined in the argument. But Job hungered after what he could not define, and the transaction by which God spoke to his hunger is cloaked by the grandeur of the storm. Therefore, the Book of Job should not be prescribed as a panacea for suffering; it should be read by those who are able, somewhere away from the heart of the tempest, to savor the meanings of words.

To know the Book of Job will not forestall anguish and despair, but it may direct the experience of tragedy toward the arms of faith. The reader will not expect pat, moralistic solutions to solve the brutal riddles which confront him. Respecting the mystery under all of life, and being in some degree sensitive to the general predicament of man, one who knows Job seeks the terrain proper to his battle that he may meet his bitter hours in that honest anguish which is the first step of healing.

As a work of art, as a part of the Bible, and as a document of the inward experience of man, the Book of Job demands a response from its readers. This response is not to be held off to one side, scrupulously separate from the words of the book, as of no vital consequence. On the contrary, for the moment the reader must become a speaker in the dialogue. Throughout the years in which I have presumed to take my place in the Joban debate, I have been sometimes embarrassed by the shifting of my views. I have learned nevertheless to respect what I see at a given moment, even though one day's sufficiency may seem another day's famine.

God speaks to man as man is able to hear. When reading the Bible, one hears new notes from a familiar passage. He need not, however, discard what he once believed. The pilgrim goes from strength to strength; at every station he needs directions suitable to the immediate stage of his travels. Subsequently, he sees new horizons and takes new directions, but he understands that he has been on pilgrimage as much in his first tentative steps as when he attains the gate of sanctuary. Early insights are not so much violated as swallowed up in greater grandeur. The stationary hear nothing new from God; their immobility forfeits that splendor of pilgrimage which is the essential beauty of every scene. Like Lot's wife, defeated when she had just begun to move, they remain frozen forever in the posture of their first anxiety.

The deepening light of passing years, falling across the pages of Job, discovers deepening meanings. For this station of my pilgrimage, the word "honor" has been emblazoned over every page. I pray that this viewpoint may command the perplexing canyons and ridges of immediate moments and afford, through some gap in the range surrounding us, a glimpse of the eternal parapets of the city of our desire.

In the Book of Job honor has become something real; it expresses a strength beyond imagination. It is strong in the inwardness of man, anchored in truth intimately his own as it extends beyond him. Interpreting the demands of honor as the will of God, man inherits honor without the corrosion of pride.

On the other hand, God, as the authority of rightness, does not ignore the intuitions of man. In order to say anything, the voice from the storm demands them. God set Job on his own feet and saved him by the chastened certainties emerging from his despair. Job had to have strength within to survive the test, for God did not intrude it from without.

Faith bears the burden of committing the heart to certainties expressed in shaky human terms. Men often try to make these terms infallible so that they may escape the anguish of responsible decision and the challenge of creative living. Therefore they codify the honor of God, huddle round the emblems of past titans and wait for the shrine of their pilgrimage to drop upon them from the sky.

The Book of Job insists that cherished ideas be liable to honest examination. Nothing remains honorable which blunts and distorts the features, which dulls the eyes and deadens the ears, which obscures and erodes the identity of man. The immutable force of Spirit senses the encroaching caricature of integrity, the rot of self; it calls man into the terrible solitude where, without the drama of outward catastrophe, he may at once suffer the sharpest torments of Job.

Courage and struggle are necessary to accept truth in a changing world; honor, the ultimate tradition, outgrows from time to time the forms by which it is transmitted. Sometimes one is most faithful to the traditions of his forefathers when he discards or reshapes them. So doing, he may rekindle the holy fire which brought traditions into being. Honor is not therefore adherence to a rigid code; it is creative, forever attempting to express the unfathomable mystery of God on the stage of history.

I would be disappointed in the reader had he not for

some time been asking, "But how can this impossible idealism work in a world where compromise is necessary? Can honor exist outside a fairy-tale world of knights and dragons?"

Admittedly, the demands of honor are never completely fulfilled. Even if a man acted always by noble impulse, his misunderstanding of his fellows would lead from time to time to costly blunders. Honor, however, is endangered not so much by those who violate their own codes as by falling into irrelevance. In the gray world of "maybe" the inner demand of conscience frequently becomes so fuzzy that dishonorable deeds become an impossibility. There remains no honor to violate!

### THE HONOR OF COUNTRY

Margaret Mead, in her book *New Lives for Old*, tells how the Manus, a stone-age people in the South Sea Islands, almost completely discarded their culture and religion and set out to construct a new society based on the American model. They decided to do this, not because of the efforts of missionaries, but because of their experiences with many thousands of soldiers during World War II.

The Manus were struck by the Americans' carelessness about material things. The prodigal spending of armament suggested that these strangers had created in their homeland an inexhaustible machine of production. The easy fraternizing of the GIs, their lack of condescension, the incredible profusion of their equipment and supplies, were only part of the story.

Above all, the primitive islanders were impressed by the American concern for the lost and wounded. The devoting of countless units of equipment to rescue downed airmen and stranded Marines told the Manus that human life was of supreme importance to Americans. The sacred skulls of their ancestors were all discarded at one time as a first step toward a new civilization.

America has a tradition of honor. She has constituted herself around the idea of the worth of each man in himself and the opportunity of each to find the environment suited to his abilities. It is true that the country's traditions have been betrayed again and again, but her sons still bring failures to the tribunal of honor, correcting and developing public policy not simply on the basis of expediency but of morality. Popular concern over the ill-fated Cuban invasion as a contradiction of national tradition rather than as a tactical blunder witnesses stubborn persistence of a tradition of honor in materialistic America.

It would be presumptuous to claim that America alone enshrines a tradition of honor. Every nation of enduring strength embodies some quality of character, some identity around which the integrity of a people is built and from which a sense of national honor emerges. However, the explicit assertion of the worth of man to his status under God, as seen in the Preamble to the Constitution, lays forever upon the American people an extraordinary measure of judgment and opportunity.

The nationalism which, since World War II, has flared up all over the world takes its force not simply from a general desire for things but from underprivileged peoples' exciting suspicion that they may be somebody after all. Much of the irrationality and violence of today's struggles toward status derives from a lust for meaningful life, a force not far removed from the luminous power of honor. Of all nations, therefore, America should find in this age a challenge peculiar to her mission: while fulfilling herself she may conquer, as she never has before, by the manifestation of her incomparable standards.

We are not so much in danger of tragedy as we are of

becoming incapable of tragedy. Lacking real identity, asserting ourselves in a mad accumulation of things, bending our consciences wherever pampered appetites snuff new profits, we become pretentious nobodies. The lack of individual honor—always true of society's faceless men—is not our problem; it is the erosion of the tradition of honor that threatens us.

When we lose honor we are unable to understand the worth of man. The worst attacks upon the dignity of others are unconsciously delivered when we reveal that others do not exist for us. Unable to sense worth in people of other countries, we are amazed when they resent us. We assume no plumbing means no intelligence or self-respect! Viewing our own identity in terms of what we have, modern Americans are often literally unable to recognize real persons in other lands unless they exhibit the proper credentials of car, refrigerator, and television set.

Beyond all contrived crises of the cold war the greatest single threat to national survival is the furious resentment of "underdeveloped peoples" to American condescension. Wounds to self-respect fester deep; in the lust for revenge, sound sense, ideology, and even self-interest go out the window. It is doubtless true that Americans, because of the nobility of their traditions, are measured by a higher standard than many. But America was created by her traditions; only in their rediscovery shall she continue to exist.

### THE CHURCH'S HONOR

The terrible struggle of Job to preserve his identity beyond all social and material symbols bespeaks the responsibility of each citizen of today's world to assert within himself and toward his brothers the dignity of the human race. Should one discover, however, that his very lifeblood depended upon the rebirth of honor, he would remain helpless to create it simply for survival. Effective honor is a force in itself. Either it masters men or, being mastered by them, disappears between their clutching fingers. When honor masters men it relates itself to deity and becomes religious in nature.

The church, as the primary means by which America understands herself to relate to the God who establishes the value of each citizen and creates the standards best suited to the cultivation of individual worth, inherits a peculiar responsibility. She is commissioned to call nations continually before the tribunal of a divine will that may seem to endanger immediate national interest. This she cannot do if on one hand she is entombed in rigid ecclesiastical tradition or, on the other, she has allowed herself to take on the identity of a nationalism rooted in particularity and pride. Christian Americanism easily becomes the deification of national self-interest. It produces a respectable strength because it substitutes the immediate power of fear and self-interest for a theoretical general faith which, in itself, never really asserted personal value. Such honor in America is really self-created and local because it does not derive from the Creator God who loves Indonesians and Afghans as he loves Nebraskans. Expressive of a Baal of spacious skies and amber waves of grain, the national identity which refuses to submit itself to the demands of the God of all skies and oceans cannot expect his protection in collision with other such identities.

The church does not exist to serve the nation, but to save souls. She can do neither, however, unless she becomes the church of God, existing in and through his will above all else. Just as a man can best be a friend to his neighbor when he values honesty and justice more than his neighbor, so the church can only perform her role for a nation when she acknowledges a Sovereignty greater than the nation itself.

However, many who profess loyalty to a God beyond nation delude themselves into supposing that insensitivity to the beliefs and practices of others constitutes Christian love. Not caring enough about their own faith to suppose that it really makes any difference, emancipated Christians are little concerned whether others agree with them or not. Those whose convictions are little related to life and so vaguely defined as impossible to debate cluster together to share the heat of faintly remembered revivals and a vague apprehension of something missing. From such groups statistics are regularly issued to assure an unconcerned world that something is really going on.

The honor of Job demands honesty above conformity. Surely there is room in the church for free souls to search with their brethren for a way to come to terms with the riddle of existence. Eliphaz, Bildad, and Zophar too often captain the companies of the saved, drawn up in indomitable array before the dead god of Irreproachable Dogma.

On the other hand, God's speech reminds the rebel that he is in the adolescence of the Spirit. He came into the world on terms other than his own. Ultimately he may rediscover himself in the submission which appropriates the solid worth of life before surrender to the inexorable logic of death.

Christians should learn from the Book of Job to respect the mystery of God. Job made the mistake of outlining heaven's alternatives. Faith always understands the unpredictable nature of God's ways with man and accepts what he wills because to experience God is to become a prophet. Knowing that his ways are not our ways, today's Christians must not be chagrined to find the deep purposes of God carried out in unlikely places through unlikely people.

When Christians do things inconsistent with the gospel

of Christ, the church must not content herself by dealing with the threat to her reputation, but ought to ask whether she has lost her identity. Worship mediates the experienced Presence that is the heart of Christian honor, but decisions which test and express integrity relate the soul to God. Decisions create the profile of Christian man. Such men understand how much is lost in a decision to extend the church in a manner inappropriate to her nature and how brotherhood based on convenience rather than the dignity of man threatens the church's identity.

Only honor sees the hidden birthright bartered away in trivial transactions. Perpetually absurd in a world of maneuver and pretension, integrity speaks up over misappropriated nickels, unimportant promises, cheating in examinations, and padded expense accounts. Honor demands painful confessions, undesirable conferences, and decisions which to other eyes can only be interpreted as senseless disloyalty to friends.

The Book of Job asks the church whether she can survive respectability. Surrounded by the protective fence of law, demonstrably sound as a business investment, soothing to the nerves, and helpful for the childern, the church seems to provide little opportunity for a man to determine for himself what God really means. When a congregation looks to building, statistics, and community status for assurance of identity, how can it be strong within? To what extent can it appeal for members by means remote from the force of the Spirit without losing power with every addition?

Yet the church amazingly represents the one point in a community where folk expect to be able to come to terms with the Almighty in love and repentance. The witness of mighty symbols, the echoes of majesty in prayer and song, the sudden unbelievable Voice addressing the heart through just another sermon, anchor the soul against the fearful moments when old idols tear loose and new life steps out barefoot. Even in the most superficial congregations, from time to time spiritual power bursts forth in the embarrassment of real conversion. A wind of forgotten power sweeps through the congregation as once again Christ is discovered to be alive and relevant.

Job could find solace neither in the traditional wisdom of the friends nor in the plausible philosophy of Elihu. His answer was not found in what God said and did but in God himself interpreted from the storm by the uncanonized revelations of agony and despair. Then Job could begin to accept the ideas of divine righteousness once so impossible for him, not indeed as adequate, but as in their necessary inadequacy rumors of the God beyond definition.

The confrontation of man by God which is the business of worship and holy fellowship cannot be created or contrived by the church. It must be granted, in the reality of the Spirit, by God himself. Fundamental to Christian conviction is the assertion that God meets man in Jesus Christ, through whom God's power becomes effective in salvation.

### THE HONOR OF CHRIST

The Book of Job therefore properly asks the church whether, at the heart of her inheritance in Jesus Christ, the question of Job is ever really met. Do the doctrines he taught, such as the hope of heaven and divine forgiveness, along with the solution of the problem of present injustice by final judgment, say what Job could not have heard from the voice from the whirlwind?

Jesus, in his teachings, did not address himself directly to the problem of the justification of God. He emphasized the coming Kingdom and the preparation of his generation for the demands of the new order. Neither he nor his contemporaries, according to our records, discussed the tragedy

151

of mankind in the philosophical frame of reference found in the Book of Job.

In a broader sense, however, Jesus is in himself a response to the outcry of Job. He participates in Job's sufferings. Interpreted from the standpoint of honor, Jesus did not suffer simply to create the recommendation of scarred hands and side, to carry out the prophecies of the Old Testament, or to be a substitute for sinful men. Valid as such aspects of the saving Christ are to his followers, Jesus in himself experienced the cross because he would not modify his ministry to suit what seemed to many patriotic and thoughtful men the demands of the times.

Jesus died because he was unwilling to sacrifice his integrity for safety and status in a lost society. He knew the will of God and understood that according to human judgment it outreached the capacities of men. At Gethsemane he chose between self and God; the power to choose beyond self came from within him. Angelic ministration followed, rather than preceded, the decision to die. His resurrection was not the reward of virtue; rather, it testified to the infinite worth, the indestructibility of Jesus in himself. The empty tomb represents the power of both God and the human spirit, measured by the infinite distance from death to life.

Since at Gethsemane Jesus stood against the coercion of friend and enemy—as well as the inclinations of natural intelligence and self-interest—and obeyed what he knew to be God's will, the Cross testifies to the power of his love for God. Jesus proclaimed the absolute worth of God, when he chose God for his own sake and forfeited life by the choice. Satan's creed can now be rewritten: "All that a man has he will give for *God*."

When Jesus chose God for himself, he testified to the honor of God. The power of honor is inward. The will of

152

God is chosen, not because of the promise of the resurrection and ascension, but because it is *God's* will, deriving from God its own radiance and establishing itself against all the temptations of Gethsemane.

In his hour of agony Jesus did not, like Job, confront God with God's alternatives. He saw that the alternatives were his own, and chose the right in a way that seems to the beholder at once free and inevitable.

When the anguish of Calvary, like the trial of Job, made it possible to choose God in himself, there came to pass in Jesus what he himself had prophesied, that "whoever loses his life for my sake will find it" (Matt. 16:25). In giving himself in single-minded passion to the right thing to do, in lonely, detached absorption with the terrestial business of God, Jesus becomes transfigured before men as he had not been on the holy mountain. Men everywhere have sensed past the insult, the dishonor, the obscene posturings, and lynch-mob hooharrahs of the passion week the majesty of very God. Having turned away from himself, Jesus displays the radiance that is the Christ, the fulfilled identity in which human honor and divine majesty become unbelievably the same.

Those who might suppose that the Christ identity is simply the creation of man misunderstand the nature of honor. God works his triumph in the freedom of Jesus so that power beyond the mechanical cause-and-effect system of the natural world might become effective.

### THE HONOR OF THE CHRISTIAN

Men who understand the cross have therefore been obsessed with the demand of the beauty of Christ. The Personality, the Presence that haunts the pages of the gospels and emerges unmistakably from Paul and James and John is the elusive goal of all Scripture. Never trapped flatly in the written word, the sublime Identity is always there. In the New Testament, every category of experience in which man has sensed the ultimate—law, sacrifice, ritual, genealogy—is pressed into service to give men some means to carry from the vision beatific their own pailful of light.

The Christ who found himself in God fulfills every role which man, in his struggle toward God, has created for himself. He is prophet without gibberish, priest without incense, king without scepter.

Since, however, Jesus manifests his glory in a choice of the will of God, man has no means by which to appropriate this glory save decision. This is why the mediation of the meaning of Jesus has been the preaching of a message telling of his death and resurrection, to which response is made in repentance or not at all. A change in life occurs, not simply because it is needed—which the sinner already knows—but because man derives from the love of God an identity which begins to express itself in radical new decisions. Man becomes at last the real self he had never been able to forget.

To see the New Testament from the standpoint of honor is to understand that salvation always has to do with the quality of the self rather than with the rescue of self as an object. Salvation is a change of heart, a rebirth for which ultimate beatitude simply provides ultimate expression. Being saved by going to heaven is analogous to seeking honor in the accumulation of things. A host of defeated humans console themselves with the hope of eventual transformation to celestial beings thronging celestial streets. Streets enough in eternity God will doubtless provide, but the people who walk them will continue to express the identity of earth's decisive moments. Earth is the laboratory of human transformation. Only in the freedom and uncertainty of human history can man change without losing himself. Those who are not of honor's fraternity fear the illumination of very heaven. Pearly gates can crush prying fingers; golden chariots can pulverize meddling feet.

Doctrines of Christianity that might be expected to answer the problem of Job are easily misused. If the pleasures of heaven can be expected to repay one for present outrage, human anguish may lose its power to stimulate re-examination of life. Shall God bribe off with candy the victims of his forgetfulness? We may silence the screams of a beaten and violated child by injections of morphine and exorcise shock from her memory by psychological treatment, but who can stand in the echo of her cries and justify by written dogma the moment in itself?

The idea that suffering automatically ennobles is easy for the comfortable. It explains somebody else's troubles. Actually, crippling and disfiguring diseases tend to destroy or distort identity. Disappointment and betrayal create bitterness and cynicism. Ruined cities spawn looters as well as heroes; starvation engenders thieves and cannibals.

The concept that suffering itself redeems man is illustrated by pathos, which is tragedy robbed of God. Pathos assaults a man's own worth, negating the inner force of honor. Self-pity insists that the center of well-being lies outside self. Suffering ennobles man only when it provides new expression for an honor prior to itself or when, as Elihu suggested, it is appropriated as a new opportunity to learn the intentions of God. The Cross is of no significance in the Christian message except as it provides the backdrop against which the honor of man and God is finally demonstrated. A Christian flees suffering for its own sake, for there is nothing in happiness inconsistent with honor.

The capacity to overcome adversity is real; it is expressive of a strength beyond imagination. The honor of the Christian derives from the discovery that what Christ declares to be the nature of God is one's own lost identity. When one submits the direction of his life to God, he inherits a new self, not so much a contradiction as a fulfillment of the old.

The standards of Christian honor do not rest fundamentally on verbal codes. To depend on codes causes man to misunderstand the inwardness of moral action and tempts him to escape coercion by manipulating regulations. The law of love, appealing to responsible selfhood, in the nature of the case must be inward.

Love is not, however, primarily emotional. It is the consistent assertion of the unconditioned, the incalculable worth of man. Such worth cannot be discovered simply in appearances, for many times the observable value of a person seems unimpressive or totally lacking. Not even my best friend's indispensability can keep me from granting him what his value before God properly demands.

Christian righteousness is simply to act on the assumption that all men are as myself. I cannot do this unaided. My inevitable self-centeredness, necessary to survival, denies that my ideal is humanly attainable. But when I experience God's love in Christ (who, when he fulfilled himself, went to a wondrous land beyond self), I experience in the peace of Gethsemane the excitement and the certainty of God. This is what I want; this is what I always should have been; this, in the grace of God, is what I am.

Honor is that form of righteousness which carries with it the power of its own performance. The justification which the apostle Paul teaches is not a distant legal transaction; it is the creation within oneself of a kind of honor which, rooted in a new experience of God, makes possible the radiance of a new self.

Through faith in Christ the saved person discovers a worth in himself which, while bearing the marks of his own strivings, extends far beyond him. The experience of God in worship and service begins to replace what had been sought in reputation and possessions. One who knows God does not need the reassurance of fame and fortune. The flourishings of trumpets, the pride and the pageantry, the color and the pomp by which man has proclaimed his citizenship in a domain beyond the gray world is no longer necessary.

Man is animal as well as spirit. Nothing happens for him which does not involve the whole self. Decisions of the spirit can only be made as they focus upon an immediate transaction which, insignificant as Moses' one sin, becomes the theater of destiny. Mouthing the word "honor" does nothing at all. Honor exists when one dares its implications; he suddenly discovers himself carried by unsuspected wings and at peace with the wholeness of things.

The apprentice of honor must not be dismayed at the blunders made in his first steps toward soundness. In his animal nature reft of instinct, he has to borrow the hero's impulse. Honor is not natural to him; he can easily be forgiven uneasiness with a new vocabulary and unfamiliar new weapons. Yet the first struggling motion upward when the spiritual novice meets God, the first impulse toward beauty and wholeness, are prophetic of mysterious grace and awesome power.

Transactions of honor nourish and adorn the self. They are opportunities for the emergence of that which is splendid in the human spirit, released in the holy fearlessness of faith. Enthralled by the enormous Something embracing all their lives, men are free to be themselves. Like Moses of old, who bore from the presence of God a radiance of which he was unaware, honorable men unknowingly illumine the earth when they struggle up from their knees to battle dragons visible only to their integrity.

They illumine the earth because so far as they are concerned they do what is necessary for them to do. Their devotion, born of intent concern with ultimate right, interprets the character of God by the brightest colors of the human spectrum and brings rapture side by side with judgment to bear on human insufficiency.